Y0-DOM-810

LIVING TOGETHER IN KNOWLEDGE

What Husbands and Wives
Can Learn About Marriage
From Each Other

Don McWhorter
and
Jane McWhorter

Publishing Designs, Inc.
Huntsville, Alabama

Quantity discounts are available from:

Publishing Designs, Inc.
P. O. Box 3241
Huntsville, Alabama 35810

Cover design and art by Phyllis Alexander

Printed in the United States of America

Library of Congress Cataloging-in-Publication Data

McWhorter, Don, 1932-
    Living together in knowledge.

    1. Marriage—United States. 2. Communication in
marriage. 3. Marriage—Religious aspects—Christianity.
I. McWhorter, Jane, 1935-   . II. Title.
HQ734.m446   1988   646.7'8   88-18510
· ISBN 0-929540-00-X

95 94 93 92 91 90 89 88   5 4 3 2 1

CONTENTS

INTRODUCTION

Marriage is a universal practice. Nothing else in the history of man has ever been so popular. Nearly everybody gets married yet nobody has to. It is a choice consciously made In past ages the choice was made by someone other than the marriage partners themselves. This is still true in some places in the world today. But it is still a choice.

Nothing as popular as marriage has ever been beset with such problems. Marriages are failing at an alarming rate. The average couple can look around their circle of acquaintances and know that the probability is strong that two out of every five of those couples will not remain married. Of course others in that group are observant also, including in their observation the average couple just mentioned. No couple is merely an onlooker; they are also a part of the statistical reality. Nobody has an ironclad, no-fail marriage. The possibility of failure is there for everyone. That must be a sobering realization. If it isn't, then we are destined to repeat our failures.

But marriage was not planned for failure. It was created for happiness. Anything with universal practice has a common beginning. The beginning of marriage was in the creation week. God said, "It is not good that man should be alone" (Genesis 2:18). That conclusion caused the creation of Eve, the marriage of Adam and Eve, and God's exclamation that marriage was "very good" (Genesis 1:31).

From that beginning you read beautiful love stories like the love between Isaac and Rebecca, Jacob and Rachel, and the hauntingly beautiful Song of Solomon. Though unmarried himself, Paul was used by the Holy Spirit to picture this beautiful love between husband and wife as a type of the love between Christ and the church (Ephesians 5:22-33). The church is described in all her glory as "a bride adorned for her husband" (Revelation 21:2). It is said to be heaven come down to this earth (Matthew 18:3).

What has happened? Where has mankind gone wrong? In too many instances this heaven on earth has been made a living hell. Why? The answer is obvious. Society has left the original pattern designed by God. He made the model and gave us instructions that would enable us to reproduce it. We have kept the idea and discarded the directions. The assembly line has gone awry.

Hopefully, this study will enable us to see the mistakes society has made and call us back to the "old paths." Surely we are tired of the tears, hurts, costs, and unhappiness of failure and are hungry for the joys, excitements, satisfactions, and fulfillment of success. If ever the need existed for a Restoration Movement, the need exists now in marriage. We pray this book may be a step in that direction. It is our aim not only to help restore and rebuild broken marriages and to assist young couples in seeking to form a happy and successful marriage from the beginning but also to aid the many couples who have ailing marriages or weak points in their structures to find healing and strength by studying and growing together.

HOW TO BE HAPPY
THOUGH MARRIED

1

With the introduction of sin into the world, man has had multitudes of problems to deal with and solve. Dealing with problems involves asking questions and seeking answers to those questions. Whether or not the problem is solved depends on asking the right questions and finding the right answers.

Many of man's most basic questions center around the home. Intended originally for man's ultimate good and highest expression of physical and emotional happiness, it has become, in many instances, the source of his greatest disappointment and unhappiness. Contrary to common conception, marriage is not made in heaven. Instead, it is sent down in kit form with a complete construction and maintenance manual. With God's instruction and a "toll free number" to call for additional help, man builds with hard work and prayer. Properly built, it can be *a heaven on earth*; improper building can result in *a living hell*.

What went wrong? God's beautiful dream has become to many a living nightmare. As suggested in the beginning, sin is the major problem. It manifests itself in many forms. Because sin wears a mask, we often do not recognize it for what it is. Another problem is man's propensity to seek the answers on his own. Human wisdom, parading under many titles and impressive sounding names, proposes many solutions. In this problem, though, as in most others *when all else fails read the instructions*. We could save ourselves much grief and heartbreak by reading the instructions from God first.

When I stated that marriage is not made in heaven, I did not want to leave the impression that God had nothing to do with it. To the contrary, the entire matter was of God's desire and design. Man was never consulted. God made the decision of marriage for man and gave it to him as a divine gift. Though divine in design and purpose, it nevertheless is of the earth and involves two very different human beings becoming *one*. Because of the humanity of man, there were problems to be solved in that very first marriage. Could we expect less today?

Today's problems, however, seem to be multiplying. I know the words *marriage* and *home* are loaded with connotative meanings for all of us. Many times they are idealized and we have only a dreamy conception of what they really mean. If these words draw a picture in your mind of *The Waltons* or *The Little House on the Prairie*, your concept is miles removed from the situation that exists in the real world.

The home today is in trouble, *big* trouble. It is under fire from without. Many "experts" are attacking the home as if it were public enemy number one. Most secular bookstores display volumes telling us the home is outdated, outmoded, and has served its need. Others preach the philosophy that it was never needed to begin with. Still others proclaim it can be saved only by making drastic changes. Some idea of what this means can be seen in one of the planks of the platform of one of our major political parties just a few short years ago when the proclamation was issued: "We endorse the home *in all its various forms.*"

The home is also on fire from within. With verbal, emotional, and physical abuse at an all-time high; with the number of divorces growing with the passing of each year; with remarriage not uncommon even for the fourth or fifth time; with millions of latch-key children; with the astronomical growth of unwed women giving birth; with a large segment of the children of this generation living in a one-parent home; with the leading cause of death for children under the age of five being physical violence at home; with suicide being the second leading cause of death among teenagers; with twenty percent of all law officers killed in the line of duty slain while answering a call due to domestic violence; need I say again that the home is in *big* trouble? With these kinds of problems, a recent study on the home conducted by Rhode Island University concluded: "Aside from a riot or warfare the most dangerous place in the world to be is at home."

If ever there were a time to get back to basics, now is that time. The story is told of Vince Lombardi, famous football coach, when he was coaching the Green Bay Packers. One Sunday afternoon he watched his team being badly beaten by a much inferior team. Afterward, in the locker room, he called for a meeting of all the players early on Monday morning. When the meeting was called to order that morning, Lombardi is said to have stated: "Today we go back to basics." Picking up a football he looked at that group of old pros and still green rookies and said, "Gentlemen, this is a football." You can't get more basic than that! Someone needs to stand before this world filled with troubled marriages and say, "Ladies and gentlemen, this is a Bible!"

Early in the history of man on this earth, we see God's plan for the home and for man's happiness abandoned. In chapters four, five, and six of the book of Genesis we see the sad climax of that rebellion. God repented that He ever made man and decided to destroy man from the face of the earth. Look at the degraded condition of man: marriage solely on the basis of sex appeal, polygamy, fame based on physical achievement, constant evil thoughts. Is it any wonder that God was angry? How much different is today's world from that world of long ago? The flood was God's solution to that situation. If man would only learn! Coach Paul "Bear" Bryant of the University of Alabama used to say, "All I ask of an athlete is that he be coachable." He knew that many who were blessed with extraordinary ability would think they knew it all or would be more interested in personal accomplishment than in teamwork. But a young man of ordinary ability and the desire to learn could develop into an excellent athlete. It is the same with all of us. All that God asks is that we be coachable and remember that He is the coach! In great Bible chapters like Genesis 24, Matthew 19, Ephesians 5, Colossians 3, and

1 Peter 3, He teaches us mighty lessons on this wonderful subject.

God created three divine institutions: the home, civil government, and the church. Each is important but in many ways the home is the foundation. Without the home neither of the other institutions could exist in their present forms. In Nashville, Tennessee, there is a club known as the *So What? Club*. It is made up mostly of business and professional people and the only way to belong is by invitation. It is a prestigious organization now over one hundred years old. The club meets monthly with an assigned topic of conversation. Dramatic and animated arguments are waged on the subject but no action is ever taken. That is where the *So What?* applies. We dare not take such an attitude toward the Word of God. When God speaks on any subject we dare not say, "So What?" Yet that is what many have done with His teaching on the home.

Henry W. Grady, famous writer for the *Atlanta Journal*, was sent to Washington, D. C. to do a series of articles on "The Capital of America." On the way he was hindered by bad weather and spent the night in a farmhouse with the family which worked that farm. He observed their thanksgiving at mealtime, their family devotion built around the Bible, their prayer before retiring for the night, their love and respect for each other. He wrote his series of articles but not on Washington, D. C. Instead, he concluded that the capital of America was the family, not the government. It still is. You may say it is trite, and maybe it is, but I dare you to deny the truthfulness of it: "The hand that rocks the cradle rules the world."

We live in a world of hurting people. Perhaps we are hurting ourselves. There is help if only we will avail ourselves of it. Once a young man asked his girl friend, "If I tried to kiss you would you call for help?" She thought about that for a moment then asked, "Why? Would you need any?" We all do from time to time whether we can bring ourselves to ask for it or not. Several years ago, when our daughter was just mastering the technique of walking, she developed the habit of trying to assert her independence by simply falling limp in the grasp of her mother's hand when she did not get her way. One day we noticed that her arm was sore and she could only whimper when we touched it. Upon taking her to the doctor we discovered that her elbow was dislocated. The doctor quickly remedied that problem and we remedied the situation that caused the problem. Before the remedying she was hurting and could not ask for help. It is our fervent desire that this book will be of help to those who are hurting whether they are at the present asking for help or not. We also hope sincerely that it will help those who are not hurting to avoid those problems in marriage that cause hurt. May the full joy and blessing that God intended for the home be yours.

LOOKING BACK

1. The curse of sin has touched everything in this world.

2. Marriage is not made in heaven but on this earth.

3. God's Book provides the instructions for putting marriages together.

4. Because we have so often ignored God's teaching, marriage is in *big* trouble today.

5. Marriage is fired at from the outside and set on fire from within.

6. We dare not say, "So what?" Instead we must get back to basics.

7. Those who are hurting must seek help.

SUGGESTIONS FOR CLASS DISCUSSION
Chapter 1

1. In the lesson this statement was made: "Whether the problem is solved or not depends on asking the right questions and finding the right answers." What are some of the right questions?

2. The home was intended for man's ultimate happiness. Instead, it has been the source of much disappointment and sorrow. Cite some of those disappointments and sorrows.

3. Even though God's plan was perfect, what problems did the first home encounter?

4. What problems is the modern home facing from without?

5. The lesson mentioned a number of problems which the home is facing from within. Discuss these and add to the list.

6. If a young person has the desire to learn, coupled with only an ordinary ability, what will probably take place? What is the message to married couples?

7. What was Henry Grady's conclusion about the capital of America? Do you agree or disagree?

8. What are the limitations set upon helping a marriage if neither party is aware that help is needed? Does your marriage need help?

THE WISE BUILDER

2

In any building endeavor the proper foundation is not only the first but also the most important step in insuring the quality and stability of the entire structure. While it is true that you cannot construct a good building with shoddy material, it is also of paramount importance to recognize that, regardless of the materials used, even the finest of materials will not endure an improper foundation.

As He closed the Sermon on the Mount, Jesus illustrated the importance of a proper foundation for life in the comparison of the two houses that were built—one on the foundation of solid rock and the other on shifting, unstable sand. Nothing is said of the relative merits of the houses themselves. Both houses may have been of equal quality. The house built on the sand may even have been larger and, to the eye of the casual observer, more beautiful than that house constructed on the rock. In view of the differences in foundation, however, all the other details were of little importance. These houses had to face the harsh realities of life—wind, rain, flood—and what difference would the house itself make if, because of its faulty foundation, it could not survive? Even a cottage that endures is better than a mansion that collapses.

What is the proper foundation for building a life and all that pertains to it? That is the whole purpose of Jesus' story. The wise man built his house, one that would endure all the trials of life, on the words of Jesus. He not only knew what those words were but he obeyed them, using them as the blueprint for the entire structure. What he built would last because it had the right foundation (Matthew 7:25).

Recognition of the right for the existence of authority and respect for that authority in our actions is the chief building

block of society. Where there is no authority evident or no
respect for authority even when it is evident, there is chaos and
eventual destruction. It is no wonder that Jesus astounded
them with His teaching for "He taught them as one having
authority and not as the scribes" (Matthew 7:29). The scribes
spoke in terms of relativism and situation ethics. Nothing was
ever settled as a matter of firm and solid ground. Much of
what is being said today sounds like what the scribes were
saying and not what Jesus said with authority. With every
sociologist, psychologist, psychiatrist, counselor, and preacher
presenting his own opinion and with the rampant views of
humanism being taught in public schools in classes ranging
from science to history to home economics, is it any wonder
that even for those seeking proper information there is bewil-
derment?

Early in His public ministry the Jewish rulers asked Jesus,
"By what authority are you teaching these things and who
gave you this authority?" These are the most basic questions
in life and finding the right answers is of utmost importance.
The authority of Jesus was the authority of God and was given
Him by God. The authority of God, respect for it, and obedience to it must be the foundation for living and building. That
is true for the church, for government, and for the home. God
is the great architect who conceived the idea and drew up the
blueprints for the home. For the home to be properly built and
thus meet His approval, it must be built on His authority and
follow His specifications:

1. Both partners must be eligible for marriage in God's
   sight. There can be no marriage unless it is scriptural;
   neither can have another marriage to which they are
   scripturally bound (Matthew 19:1-9).

2. There must be lifetime commitment (Romans 7:1-4).
   It is a vow that cannot be broken (Numbers 30:2;
   Ecclesiastes 5:4).

3. The two must become one in a shared identity (Genesis
   2:23,24).

Teresa

4. There must be absolute sexual faithfulness (Exodus 20:14; Galatians 5:19; Titus 2:4,5).

5. Each must understand and accept the roles God has assigned male and female, husband and wife (1 Corinthians 11:3; Ephesians 5:21-23; Colossians 3:18,19; 1 Peter 3:1; Titus 2:4,5; 1 Timothy 2:15).

6. There must be genuine love of each for the other (Colossians 3:19; Ephesians 5:25; Titus 2:4).

7. God requires mutual submission to one another and mutual sharing of the loads brought on by marriage and home (Ephesians 5:21).

8. Each must provide sexual fulfillment and joy for the other (1 Corinthians 7:1-5).

9. There must be mutual respect (Ephesians 4:31,32; 1 Peter 3:1-7).

These are the foundation stones, the building blocks for successful marriage. They are straight off the original blueprint. I realize that in today's mixed up world some seem quaintly old fashioned and others appear to be realistically impossible. Remember, however, that God is the architect and He sought no advice from man. Neither does He need man's advice today. To restore the home to its original place in man's fulfillment and happiness, God's plan must be followed with no additions, deletions, substitutions, or exceptions. Remember, "Except the Lord build the house, they labor in vain that build it" (Psalms 127:1,2).

Ideally the home should be a Christian home. There is strong advice in the scriptures concerning marrying a Christian. It was that strong advice from Paul on this subject that caused many in Corinth to conclude that if a Christian were married to a non-Christian, the marriage should be dissolved. Paul's instruction in 1 Corinthians 7 is crystal clear. Such marriages, though not ideal, are, nonetheless, scriptural. Marriage does not have to be to a Christian one in order to be scriptural because even the non-Christian must accept the authority of God on marriage in order to be scripturally married. For there to be any happiness or success in marriage, everyone, whether Christian or not, must build by the plan of God. Crusty old *Inspector 12* declares, "They don't say Hanes until I say they say Hanes!" The God of heaven and ruler of this universe says, "It isn't a marriage until I say it is a marriage!" That's the only authority that counts when you decide to get married and build a home.

But a happy and successful marriage must be more than scriptural. The union of just any two people who have a scriptural right to that joint venture is no way to build a home. There are many other qualities that must be weighed. These qualities are personal in nature. Ignore them and even a marriage with a scriptural foundation will have a hard time. It may endure but it will be more of a test of endurance than the beautiful and fulfilling thing that God envisioned when He ordained it. Yet how many times do people assess the success of marriage only on these two qualities—scripturalness and endurance. While both are absolutely necessary, they do not, indeed cannot, produce a happy and thus a successful marriage. As appalled as we all are at the indecency of the divorce rate, that is by no means the only indicator of marriage failure. Many couples that stay together, for whatever reason, are doomed to a lifetime of unhappiness and regret. In many instances it was a marriage that never should have happened.

We live in a rapidly changing world. These changes affect every facet of our lives. All change is not wrong and neither is all change progress. We must never make the mistake of equating cultural and traditional qualities with scripturalness. Regardless of personal preferences, however strong they may be, we must recognize them for what they are and never elevate them to the place of scripturalness or unscripturalness. It is just as much a sin to make a law where God has not made one as it is to ignore a law God has made. It is all too easy to let personal preferences do that. The nostalgic scenario of my generation of Dad being the sole breadwinner of the household with Mom home wearing a cotton print dress with an apron and baking apple pies while all the children are busy either with school homework or work around the house is a dream of the past. It may look that way in reruns of *Leave It to Beaver* or *Lassie* but it is a far cry from the reality of today, To insist that lifestyle in that mode is the only scriptural lifestyle for families is to doom a marriage to failure before it starts. Changes that have altered lifestyles—changes like more education for women and in many different fields, women working outside the home, women earning money (sometimes even more than their husbands), husbands taking a greater part in child-rearing and house management, husbands and wives participating together in decision making—are not unscriptural and neither are they the cause of unhappiness and marital failure. Quite often it is the lack of these changes that is to blame. Let's quit using them as scapegoats and ready excuses for failure and find the real culprit. We must also avoid holding old cultural and traditional ways up to scorn and ridicule. Nothing but harm can come from either attitude. Revere and follow the teaching of God's Word for it never changes. Matters that are merely cultural and traditional will change and we must all be flexible enough to change with them, if not in practice at least in tolerance and understanding.

Every generation must have role models for nearly every endeavor in life. What are the role models for the young adults of this generation as they form their attitudes about the opposite sex and their concepts about marriage? One of the most powerful of these influences is television programing. You do not have to be a television fan yourself to know the standard fare that is being served—hardly ever the portrayal of the nuclear family at all; instead it is triangle or quadrangle, a divorce, or (usually) an arrangement of simply living together. In nearly every instance of the treatment of the nuclear family, it is held up to open ridicule and scorn, merely a joke and a bad one at that. One partner or both are depicted as adulterers. The husband and father is pictured as inept, ignorant, prejudiced, and overbearing while the wife is pictured as liberated in the worst sort of way.

The other role model for young adults is their own parents. Too often they pay lip service almost to the point of worship of the traditional past but hardly ever do they even attempt to live up to it. Most are not deeply religious and, even among the religious, there is an open disrespect and defiance of the Bible as any standard at all in marriage. Divorce has become as big a problem for church-going people as for those who make no pretense in that direction. Even where marriage has endured there is obvious unhappiness and many unresolved problems. Is it any wonder that this generation is having trouble finding the proper foundation for marriage? Where is the voice of the church? Where is the action of Christian couples setting the right example and serving as proper role models? They are badly needed.

Granting that the marriage meets the first requirement, that of scripturalness (and if it doesn't, the matter stops right here because if this demand is not satisfied nothing else can help), what are the other qualities that make up a happy, successful marriage? There are, of course, many but the outstanding ones are dominant in every good marriage. It is these we will be studying in the remaining chapters of this book.

* *WE'RE DIFFERENT!* While there are many obvious differences between any two individuals (personality, likes and dislikes, habits, etc.) the most obvious as well as the most important difference between husband and wife is their maleness and femaleness. In this they are so different as to appear almost to be from different planets. It is these differences that make marriage possible and enjoyable. It is also these differences that determine the God-given roles of each in marriage. Yet in most books, seminars, counseling sessions, and other attempts to deal with the problems of marriage and offer solutions that bring happiness and fulfillment, the differences of sexual makeup and the roles they necessitate are either ignored or openly ridiculed. Not until we learn these differences, respect them, and find joy in them will we have a happy marriage. God

decreed it so and who would question that the Creator knows best?

* *GETTING THE MESSAGE ACROSS.* As social creatures communication is a must. No relationship of any kind can exist in the absence of real communication. But communication is more than the mere exchange of information. Even strangers can do that. True communication consists of sending and receiving both verbal and non-verbal messages. It is the baring of the soul to your mate on the real and meaningful issues of your lives and your marriage.

* *I DO!* What in life can continue to live and be fruitful without commitment? It is essential in any field of endeavor. While we understand this in every other facet of life, strangely it seems never to have occurred to many that it is a primary building stone of marriage. The commitment that builds a happy marriage cannot be to the marriage alone; it must also be to the marriage partner. One committed to the marriage but not to the partner is destined for a long marriage but an unhappy one.

* *HOW TO LEAD BY FOLLOWING.* No word or concept is more misunderstood or resented in today's world than *submission.* It is a beautiful concept and absolutely essential to a fulfilling life. It is a concept that must be applied everywhere. God's command is "submitting yourselves to one another in love" (Ephesians 5:21). Submission is the most powerful weapon of change in the world. In no area of life is it more powerful than in marriage.

* *FEELINGS.* As creatures of feelings we should acknowledge that emotions are a most important part of our make-up. Recognizing them, admitting them, rejoicing in them, serving them, mastering them—all are a part of living together as husband and wife.

* *WHEN THE HOUSE IS BUILT ON THE SAND.* Recognizing and rejecting faulty building materials for the

home, especially for the foundation, is so important. With all the misinformation being disseminated by everyone from *ignoramus* to *expert*, recognizing the counterfeit is not easy. The pressures of the world around us weigh heavily on our marriage. We must pay the price of a good foundation if our home is to stand.

* *IDENTITY CONFLICTS—WHICH AM I?* Not only knowing but also accepting your uniqueness as an individual is vital to personal happiness and success as well as to the joy and victory of the home in today's world. Learning to resolve these conflicts is essential.

* *WHEN THERE IS NETWORK TROUBLE.* High on the list of trouble causers in marriage is the breakdown of communication. Without communication how can we relay our pleasures and joys? How can we seek solutions to our problems? Lines of communication must be kept open at all costs.

* *WHEN "I DO" BECOMES "I DON'T."* When commitment dies the marriage dies. It may be years before it is laid to rest but those years are only spent marking time. The only question to be answered is, "When and where will we bury the corpse?" We must work at commitment. While it is a once-for-all-time matter, it also needs periods of refreshing. Sometimes commitment needs a dose of recommitment—both to the marriage and to the partner.

* *WHEN "I WILL" BECOMES "I WON'T."* Sad indeed is the spectacle of two living as one flesh without the beautiful balm of submission. Gone is care and concern and the lovely things that thrillingly accompany them. Left are only sheer determination and guts. While these qualities are not to be cheapened, they make a poor fare for marriage when they are the only entrees on the menu.

* *WHEN EMOTIONS CONTROL.* Emotions are great and it takes the full range of the octave to make beautiful music in the soul. But they must be servants, not masters. In their God-given place they serve a great function. When

they usurp scripture, reason, commitment, submission, and other rightful partners in our makeup, they become demons of destruction.

IN CONCLUSION

1. All of us are in the construction business. How long our structure endures depends upon the foundation and the building materials.

2. Respect for proper authority is the basic building block of society.

3. The ultimate authority in marriage is God's Word.

4. A happy and successful marriage must be more than scriptural.

5. A happy marriage must fulfill roles, provide communication, show submission, and be full of feelings.

SUGGESTIONS FOR CLASS DISCUSSION
Chapter 2

1. In Matthew 7:24-29 is there any indication as to which house was better in quality or beauty? What was the only redeeming quality?

2. The houses in Matthew 7 both had to face the harsh realities of life—wind, rain, and floods. What sort of hard realities does the home face today? How are these different from the ones faced a century ago?

3. What is the only enduring foundation for life and for the home?

4. What happens when there is no authority or respect for authority?

5. What does Matthew 7:29 teach concerning the authority of Jesus? Did the scribes have any authority? How did they teach?

6. How does humanism challenge the authority of God?

7. From whom did Jesus receive His authority? What must be our source of authority?

8. According to Matthew 19:1-9 can there be a scriptural marriage unless both partners are eligible?

9. Compare Romans 7:1-4, Numbers 30:2, and Ecclesiastes 5:4 in discussing the seriousness of a commitment.

10. What are some ways in which a husband and a wife become one?

11. Contrast the views of the world regarding sexual faithfulness to Exodus 20:14, Galatians 5:19, and Titus 2:4,5.

12. How do the roles of husbands and wives differ? (See 1 Corinthians 11:3; Ephesians 5:21-23; Colossians 3:18,19; 1 Peter 3:1; Titus 2:4,5; and 1 Timothy 2:15.) Discuss the world's view of roles as contrasted with these scriptures.

13. Compare the commands of genuine love found in Colossians 3:19, Ephesians 5:25, and Titus 2:4 to the social standards of the first century.

14. What is the mutual submission commanded in Ephesians 5:21?

15. Which aspect of marriage is taught in 1 Corinthians 7:1-5?

16. Mutual respect is instructed in Ephesians 4:31,32 and 1 Peter 3:1-7. In what sort of respect did the world hold women at the time these words were penned?

17. If a Christian is married to an unbeliever, is the marriage a scriptural one according to 1 Corinthians 7? Why?

18. Discuss some of the changes which have altered the lifestyles of both individuals and families. Is this good or bad?

19. The two primary role models for young couples are television and their own parents. What is the effect of each?

WE'RE DIFFERENT

3

"And the Lord God said, It is not good that the man should be alone; I will make an help meet for him" (Genesis 2:18).

God could have made another Adam as a companion to the crowning glory of all His creations. But the first man needed a being completely different to complement or complete those qualities which were lacking in him. The simple words "male and female created he them" (Genesis 2:18) are powerful indeed. Jehovah never intended for men and women to be alike.

The Law of Moses recognized the fact that a newly married couple needed some time alone to become adjusted to the characteristics of one another. Hence, the new husband did not have to go to war nor be charged with any business for one year after the wedding (Deuteronomy 24:5).

In the New Testament Peter placed upon the shoulders of men the responsibility to "dwell with them according to knowledge" (1 Peter 3:7). Through inspiration Peter penned a command as binding as any other within the pages of the scriptures. As the leader of the home, husbands were told to take the time and effort to learn all about their wives. We should understand both our physical and emotional differences because we are different!

A lack of knowledge and interest can undermine a marriage and lead to its downfall. Good relationships don't just happen; they are nurtured. Building a good marriage never ends. Having too much pride to seek help produces destruction (Proverbs 29:23).

Real love, agape love, understands the needs of someone and seeks ways to fulfill those needs. But it cannot be done without knowledge. In this respect a marriage can be compared to the growing of flowers. Neglect only portends certain death. Good intentions without knowledge can also lead to ruin. For example, plants can be chemically burned if too much fertilizer is used. Time is needed to learn what sort of care is needed for each particular one.

A woman does not know what it is like to be a man because she has never been one. And a man hasn't the slightest idea of how it feels to be a woman! Both must patiently and gently explain their differences to one another. The sooner they can begin, the better. The process is a slow one.

PHYSICAL DIFFERENCES

Aside from the more obvious sexual differences in male and female, there are many other physical differences that are unknown to most couples.

Much research has been done in this field. The following facts are largely based upon the findings of Dr. Paul Popenue, founder of the American Institute of Family Relations in Los Angeles.

1. The hormones of each sex are different. Those of women are more numerous.

2. The makeup of the blood differs. A woman's blood has more water and twenty percent fewer red cells, which circulate the oxygen supply throughout the body. Due to this condition, it is the female who tires more easily and has the greater tendency to faint.

3. Men and women differ in the combination of their chromosomes. This is a basic factor in the development of male and female.

4. A man's metabolism is normally higher than that of a woman. (That is the reason he is allowed more calories on a diet!)

5. A woman's thyroid is more active than that of a man. Hence, the female is more prone to develop a goiter.

On the other hand, the more plentiful secretions of this gland are responsible for her smooth skin and the layer of subcutaneous fat that gives her body feminine curves. It also triggers her emotional tendency to laugh and cry more easily than men do.

6. Since a woman's metabolism slows down less, she can withstand high temperatures better than a man can. Due to her more active thyroid, she has a greater resistance to cold.

7. The internal organs differ in size. Surprisingly enough, it is the female who has the larger stomach, liver, kidneys, and appendix. However, the male's lungs are larger, making his breathing capacity much greater.

8. Muscle tissue accounts for forty percent of a man's body weight but only twenty-three percent of that of a woman. Naturally, he surpasses her in brute strength.

9. A man's heart beats seventy-two times a minute whereas the woman's average rate is eighty. Her blood pressure is ten points lower than that of a man, and she has less tendency to high blood pressure during her child-bearing years.

10. A woman has greater constitutional vitality than a man and consequently outlives him by three or four years in this country.

11. On IQ tests a man scores higher on math and abstract reasoning. A woman is more adept in language, reading, grammar, and all verbal skills.

12. A woman is more sensitive to sounds, tastes, smells, and touches.

The physical discrepancies between the sexes are minimal when compared to the emotional! The seat of emotions, the hypothalamic region situated above the pituitary gland in the middle of the brain, is different. Consequently, men and women have different feelings.

A WOMAN'S FEELINGS

Please take the time to look deeply within me. I may say something because it is the proper expression of what is expected. Words have meaning only as they are interpreted by the one who speaks and also by the one who hears. Look at my face. Listen to the tone of my voice. Read my eyes. Walk behind the shells of words and search for my true feelings.

Like you, I have some very basic needs. If they are fulfilled, I cannot do enough for you. I will do far more if you show me love and appreciation than I will do from a sense of duty or because you demand it.

If my basic needs are not met and my spirit has been wounded, I will probably defend myself in some rather obnoxious ways. I may rebel by being stubbornly defiant. I may nag. I may give you the silent treatment.

As I tell you of my needs, I bare myself and stand before you emotionally naked. If you ridicule me or even treat my thoughts lightly, I will probably close the door to my heart and never again invite you to enter.

1. Much has been said about woman's intuition, but scientific research has shown that it is not a myth. A Stanford University research team composed of neuropsychologists McGuiness and Triban has substantiated the fact that women perceive subliminal messages faster and more accurately than men do. I not only hear words. I also glean much from facial expressions and touch.

2. A house is far more than brick, lumber, and glass. It is also an extension of myself. As a little girl I played house, papering rooms made of grocery boxes, making curtains, and arranging miniature furniture. The appearance of my home now is important to me because it *is* me. Buying new furnishings is much like purchasing new clothes for my body. When you thoughtlessly mess up my house, I feel as if you have rubbed mud all over my face. When you criticize my house, you are,

in effect, criticizing me. It may be difficult for you to understand; but a move from my house, my security, tears me from my identity.

A house shelters people within its four walls. Just as I lovingly cared for my dolls as a child, even now I gain a great deal of my self-esteem through my family.

Whereas your sense of worth is primarily based upon achievement (your career and sports, which are extensions of your own boyhood), please try to understand the tremendous part my house and family have upon my own identity.

3. Although it may seem paradoxical in view of such a strong attachment to my house and family, please be aware of the tremendous pressures which I face in running that home. Do not take my responsibilities lightly. Both physically and emotionally I often feel drained. The continuous demands of small children can eat into the core of an adult nervous system. I never feel caught up. Constant panic becomes a way of life, especially if it is truly necessary for me to work outside my home. The realization that you care and are concerned is most assuring to me. It has been said that the wife and mother sets the tone for the home, but it is you who set the tone for my sense of well-being.

4. The media has undermined my position for years. I have important ideas to share. Ask my opinion in various areas. Respect my intelligence. I am a person of worth.

5. I may not be knowledgeable in all your areas of interest. The sports in which you actively engage may hold no appeal to me. I may not even know all the rules for the games which you watch for hours on television. If, however, you make me feel that I am the most important person in your life and that these games are not my rivals, I will hold no resentment over your viewing or participating in such events.

6. While I very greatly appreciate all the things which you give me, the most cherished present is the gift of yourself. Take me out for an evening (even for no special occasion) and make me feel like a queen. My reaction may literally astound you.

7. I love inexpensive sentimental surprises.

8. My natural tendencies do not lean toward mechanical repair. Please be observant and fix the little break-downs around the house without my mentioning them.

9. I want you to lead me but I do not want you to domi-nate me. Cherish me (Ephesians 5:29), realizing that I am not emotionally able to handle some things. I need a strong, tender, sensitive, and understanding husband to lean upon.

10. In view of the items mentioned above, this suggestion may seem a bit puzzling. While sincerely desiring your loving protection, I do not want to be smothered by your control. Please give me some freedom. Do not make me account for every minute of time or for every penny of money. You have every right to the same privilege.

11. Peter refers to woman as "the weaker vessel" (1 Peter 3:7), meaning literally that she is, by nature, the more sensitive of the two. Realize that I am naturally more vulnerable to criticism than men. Please do not cut me down in public. Instead, find something for which to praise me.

12. My moods do not always remain constant. They fluc-tuate with the supply of hormones in my body. When I do not seem to be myself, please be patient and under-standing.

13. Whereas men are generally more interested in facts, logic, and issues, I am more concerned with emotions, people, and their feelings. Intimate relationships are

important to me. For example, we women are the ones who are usually more interested in courses on marriage and other relationships involving people.

14. Love is a many splendored thing with many, many facets. A woman needs time in order to be sexually aroused. I respond to gentleness and tenderness, an aura of romance, a closeness to my husband as a person. If you are willing to invest the time and effort, you may be overwhelmed by my response.

A MAN'S FEELINGS

Though we are *one flesh* and live our lives together in the same house, share the same bed, and eat our meals together, we are so completely different that we almost live in two different worlds. Only God could have made two so different and yet so compatible and so necessary to each other for happiness and completeness.

For many years of your life you function on a biological time clock. From young manhood through old age I am basically the same from day to day and year to year. Your entire makeup is geared for living in a world of emotions. My world is basically factual—black and white—plain words and simple actions. This does not mean that I am incapable of feeling emotions. It does mean that my feelings are more openly seen and expressed. I am not coy and find it difficult to express myself in such a manner.

The world in which I live is one judged by words and actions. In my work I take criticism and meet quotas. I do not consider criticism to be a lack of love or understanding but rather just a part of the territory. I may sometimes treat you the same way, forgetting that you take such things personally and therefore very emotionally.

Though I communicate with words, I tend to do so in fewer words than do you and without the more subtle forms of communication you deem so valuable. You ask, "Do you love me?'' and I'm prone to say, "You have a house, a car, three meals a day, don't you?'' That is my way of saying "I love you,'' and I need to know that you see that and appreciate it. You want cards and flowers and perfume. Those are the things with which I am supposed to say, "I love you.'' It takes me awhile to realize that you expect *both*. To me houses and cars and food and clothing are pretty big things and are powerful ways of saying, "I love you.'' Forgive me if sometimes I forget the other. We see them in a different light. Realize that I am expressing my love sometimes in ways you fail to grasp.

Even though I live in a harder and harsher world, there is still something of a little boy that continues to live in me. I love to *play* and find time spent with other men fulfilling to my sense of manhood. I may protest but I also find a little "mothering" comforting and reassuring at times. I am expected to understand your emotions. Please understand mine, too.

Sexually I have no mountains and valleys such as you experience. Romance does not play nearly the role in my life as it does in yours. Please understand that the same God who made you also made me. Sexual love is a basic part of our relationship. When we have differences I feel that this is the way to resolve them—to *make up*. When you are cold to my advances, I fail to realize that to you this can come only *after* we have resolved our differences and *made up*. Because of my basic nature and make-up, I resent your attention to other men and any attempts at flirting or displaying affection. To you it may all seem very innocent but to me it is deadly serious; it is dynamite.

I find it hard to ask for help or to admit mistakes. Expecting me to stop and ask directions while trying to drive somewhere is almost like asking the impossible. Give me time and I will find it. It may take two or three hours but I will do it by myself. And never mind that we have just passed the last restaurant for fifty miles. Driving on that fifty more miles is much easier than turning around and going back two blocks. After all, that would be two blocks out of the way, wouldn't it?

Men find it hard to talk in the dark while lying down. If you want to talk about something, make a pot of coffee and pull out a chair at the kitchen table and say, "Let's talk." With a man, ninety-nine times out of a hundred, when he is in a prone position with a pillow under his head and the room completely dark, he is ready to go to sleep. Please don't expect what is nearly impossible for him under the circumstances—conversation. It is just very unnatural to a man to put those two together. Please do not take that as disinterest in you or in any problem you might want to discuss. Instead try changing the circumstances.

A home may be a man's castle but he knows and wants a woman to rule it (1 Timothy 5:14). He does not mind chairs you can't sit on or rugs you can't walk on, and he appreciates the cleanliness and orderliness a woman brings to his home. But he also desires one little corner, just a spot, to call his own that does not always have to be neat and orderly and picked up. Let me have that.

Simon Peter says that we are to live with each other "according to knowledge" (1 Peter 3:7). How could we better know about each other than by openly and simply telling one another who we are and how we function—what makes us tick. Hopefully all husbands and wives will do this, realizing both happiness and heaven depend on it!

INDIVIDUAL DIFFERENCES

The differences mentioned previously are those characteristic of males and females respectively. Most men's thoughts run in one channel whereas those of women take an entirely different course.

There is another set of differences that has absolutely nothing to do with men and women. These differences are entirely individual. For example, a man may spend all the money he lays his hands on. His wife wants to save every dime. Or the situation may be reversed. The wife is the spender and the husband is the saver. It is not a matter of the way men or women act as a group but rather individual characteristics.

It is amazing how opposites seem to attract. One pouts while the other explodes. A loner is frequently teamed with a sociable partner who never meets a stranger. An advocate for *a place for everything and everything in its place* winds up with one who could care less where the dirty clothes are thrown or simply dropped. The always punctual partner inevitably is yoked for life with the procrastinator who never does anything on time.

Differences in marriage can be better tolerated if they can only be understood.

1. The very traits of character which we find to be annoying under the stress of everyday living are usually the ones which attracted us in the first place. For example, if you are cool, composed, and always in complete control of yourself, you were no doubt fascinated by someone who was expressive (even in a volatile sense), warm, and passionate. If you had always allowed money to flow through your fingers like water, you were naturally attracted to someone who possessed what you lacked—the ability to live frugally.

2. Realize that your mate possessed these character traits either by genes, by family environment, or a combination of the two long before you ever met. The characteristics can be modified and adapted somewhat, but the basic core of the personality seldom changes.

3. The key lies in understanding the feelings of one another and in communicating one's own needs in a nonthreatening manner. A loner can become more sociable but some degree of solitude will always be required. A spender may learn to manage money more wisely, but the money will probably never find its way to a savings account.

Since the differences are what attracted you in the first place, they are good. But they must be seen through the eyes

of two responsible adults.

The adage "You can't have your cake and eat it, too," will have to be changed to: "You wanted your cake. You've got it and now you'll have to eat it."

Husbands and wives should accept one another as human beings. Each person has a set of good as well as bad characteristics. Most marriages could be strengthened if the partners would only rid themselves of self-righteous attitudes and devote some time to looking for the good qualities and strengthening those by praise.

A SUMMARY

1. Men and women are two completely different creatures.

2. Living together happily in marriage means *both* must LEARN to do so.

3. Physical differences are obvious and can be easily learned. Emotional differences are another matter. There is even a larger gulf and both have a *lot* to learn.

4. Most of what we need to learn we can learn simply by observing and listening to each other. The communication is there; it just needs interpretation.

5. We must love each other in order to be patient while we are learning.

SUGGESTIONS FOR CLASS DISCUSSION
Chapter 3

1. Adam was placed in a nearly perfect environment. Why was it not good for him to be alone (Genesis 2:18)?

2. Under the Law of Moses what special privileges did a newly married couple enjoy (Deuteronomy 24:5)?

3. What command is given in 1 Peter 3:7? Is this admonition any less binding than other commandments? Why do most fail to heed these divine instructions?

4. Why is a good marriage not accidental?

5. What produces destruction according to Proverbs 29:23?

6. Compare the nurturing of a marriage to the nurturing of plants. Add your own point of view.

7. Thirteen facts were presented concerning the physical differences between men and women. Assign each one to a class member for reading and comments.

8. Is woman's intuition a myth or a reality? What difference does it make in a marriage?

9. In what ways does a woman's concept of a house differ from that of a man? How is it an extension of herself?

10. Discuss the pressures which a woman faces in the running of a home. What parallel pressures does a man face?

11. What is the key in preventing a woman from feeling resentment over her husband's viewing or participating in sports?

12. What gift does a woman cherish most? What does she mean by *inexpensive sentimental surprises*?

13. When a woman says that she wants to be led but not dominated, what does she mean? Discuss the cherishing nature of subjection as it is explained in the fifth chapter of Ephesians.

14. What is the meaning of the term *the weaker vessel* in 1 Peter 3:7? Does it imply that woman is inferior to man?

15. How do a woman's moods differ from those of a man?

16. Discuss the implications of this statement: "Whereas men are generally more interested in facts, logic, and issues, women are more concerned with emotions, people, and their feelings."

17. How does a man's biological time clock differ from that of a woman?

18. In what way does a man's concept of criticism differ from that of a woman?

19. What is one of the strongest ways that a man finds to communicate the feeling of love? Do most women realize that men are using this method to express their feelings?

20. Why does a man, in view of his masculinity, still desire some "mothering"?

21. A man views sexual love as a means of reconciliation when there has been a disagreement. A woman feels differences must first be resolved before there can be sexual enjoyment. How can this contrast present problems?

22. Why are most men hesitant about asking for directions?

23. Discuss the best times for communicating feelings. How can husbands and wives "dwell together according to knowledge" unless they take the necessary time to explain their feelings to one another?

24. The previous differences have been primarily masculine and feminine characteristics. What part do individual differences have in a marriage? (For example, a neat person is attracted to someone who is very untidy. A loner is paired with a sociable partner. A spender marries someone who is very frugal.) Give your own examples and discuss the implications in marriage.

GETTING THE MESSAGE
ACROSS

4

Communication is the life blood of any joint endeavor. It is to love and marriage what the blood stream is to the human body. Like faith, love that is not expressive and communicative is dead (James 2:24). Communication is the means of revealing your true self in order that others can accept the real you and understand the message you are conveying.

The value of communication to life itself is seen all around us. Radio, television, the printed page—all are efforts to communicate with the masses in a general way and with each one in particular. Telephones and postal service open avenues of more personal communication. Group conversations and one-to-one communications are daily events in the lives of most of us.

The need for communication is seen by the government, industry, school, church, and every organization around us. One of the greatest fears of government is a pre-emptive strike by another nation with a nuclear weapon which would make communication with its own defense forces impossible. Industry and education are constantly holding seminars on the need for better communication. One of the chief objectives of the school is to teach a form of communication. In sports, the coach is constantly communicating with the players, sending both verbal and non-verbal messages even while the game is in progress. One of the chief concerns of the church is communication. Elders must communicate with each other and with the congregation. The congregation must communicate within itself and with the community in which it is found. The Great Commission is a charge to communicate God's love and grace to a lost world and to await the response in conversion of souls that are lost.

Because marriage is the most intimate of all earthly relationships, is it any wonder that communication is so necessary
to its health and happiness? In searching for a suitable illustration of the relationship between husband and wife, Paul chose
the relationship between Christ and the church (Ephesians
5:21-31). Christ, the head, took the initiative and communi-
cated His love for the church by dying for her. The communicative response of the church was to love and obey. That same
open and loving communication must exist between husband
and wife. When lines of communication are blocked, the flow
of life ceases and the marriage dies. The corpse may be pre-
served for several years but there is no life there. The most
common response in today's world is just to bury the corpse of
marriage and look for new life elsewhere. The death of the
marriage by the failure of communication is sin. To use it as
an excuse to bury that marriage and seek a new life in another
marriage is compounded sin (Matthew 19:1-9).

Let's look now at some ways in which communication can
be improved and marriage can be made the beautiful and
deeply satisfying relationship God intended it to be.

DEFINITION

Two people can scarcely be expected to regularly practice
a skill if they do not even know what it is. This facet of the
marriage union is probably the most talked about, the most
written about, and the least understood of all phases of the
relationship. Most people do not know what it is, how to get
it, or even whether or not they would like it if they had it.

You have probably heard the story about the woman who
sought the services of a lawyer in her desire to obtain a divorce
from her husband. With pen and pad in hand he began to ask
some preliminary questions:

"Do you have grounds?" he asked.

"Yes," she replied, "about an acre."

Somewhat startled by her reply and thinking she had misunderstood the question, the lawyer then asked, "Do you have

a grudge?''

"No," was her simple response. "But we do have a beautiful carport," she added.

Completely frustrated at this point, the attorney probed, "Does he beat you up?''

In a straightforward manner she answered, "Never! I get up before he does every day.''

In exasperation the counselor said, "Lady, just tell me in simple language why you want a divorce.''

Her reason was stated in simplicity: "Because I've been married to that man for sixteen years and he cannot carry on an intelligent conversation.''

Does that little story sound far-fetched? It may be closer to truth than we realize. One of the most common complaints heard from couples in troubled marriages is, "We just can't communicate." That's not really what they mean. The truth of the matter is they cannot communicate effectively. It is impossible not to communicate because all the negative things we think of as substitutes for communication are, in reality, just poor means of communication. Someone says, "My husband won't say a word. He just sits there and stares." Both silence and facial expression, though non-verbal, are means of communication. Once a father punished his young teenage son for swearing and accompanied the punishment with the admonition to never do that again. Hurting more in pride than in body the boy glared at his father, stalked out of the room, and slammed the door. His father immediately called him back and administered another whipping. "Why?" his son demanded. "I never said a word!" His father's reply was, "But you slammed the door and that's what I call 'wooden swearing.'" Yes, even in the absence of words, that boy was communicating but in a very negative and destructive way.

There are levels of communication in the marriage union just as there are in any other relationship. In the most meaningful sense, however, true communication is simply an indepth sharing of feelings between two people as they stand emotionally naked before one another and search for a solution to a problem. It is the peeling away of the layers of veneer and facade that we have used for self-protection until we bare our souls to one another, warts and all.

LEVELS OF COMMUNICATION

The deepest level of communication cannot be expected as soon as the vows are spoken although a foundation ideally should have been laid during courtship days. It is inevitable that any marriage will have some problems. The closeness of daily living, with its thorns and rocks in the pathway, demands the ventilation of irritations in an acceptable manner. The crack in the foundation of marriage may seem insignificant at first. As the years go by, however, problem will pile up on top of problem until the crack widens to an alarming degree. Then one day a problem will appear that may not seem too devastating in and of itself. Yet it may well be the proverbial straw that broke the camel's back simply because earlier problems were allowed to fester and were never adequately solved. The crack need never to be widened by accumulating problems if those disagreements can be diffused through proper communication.

The first level of communication is that of chitchat or cliches. It is simply talk about the everyday happenings of life. Usually it is pleasant and superficial and of no emotional significance. "How are you?" "Where have you been?" "I like your coat." "How's your wife?" "Nice weather, isn't it?" There is no real tension, no exposure of true feelings. It is comfortable. No one is trying to change someone else. Generally speaking, most conversation is on this level and most people can handle it with ease. There is absolutely nothing wrong with this level as long as it is not the only level upon which husband and wife can communicate. In fact, many may use this as a wall to prevent any real communication.

The second level of communication pertains to the facts and also the happenings in the lives of other people. (It sometimes borders on gossip.) "The Braves won the game." "She is having a party this week." "Did you hear what he did?" Like local newscasters, husbands and wives simply report the happenings without sharing personal feelings about them. This level is necessary. To constantly communicate on a much deeper level would be too heavy emotionally. How sad it is to see married couples eating at a restaurant in complete silence. How often we are prone to wonder, "Isn't there anything the two of you can sit there and talk about for thirty minutes?" The reading of newspapers and magazines provides food for small talk such as this. Its lightness balances the weightier matters which must be discussed from time to time. The real tragedy comes when this level is as high as a husband and wife can go in talking with one another.

The third level may be called testing the water. Instead of saying, "Let's go to the mountains on our vacation this year," the statement is phrased, "What would be your reaction to a vacation in the mountains this year?" In the latter statement the person has not risked the rejection of his own opinions or feelings in the matter. Testing tells him whether or not it is safe to pursue the matter further.

The fourth level involves stepping out to risk one's ideas and judgments on a matter. "I like this music." "I can't stand that color." "I wish you wouldn't do that." A somewhat shy person will usually retreat to safety if his ideas are not accepted. Consequently, it is not at all unusual to see a domineering mate yoked to a quiet, shy husband or wife. Perhaps the shy one meekly ventured forth with his opinion just once too often, and then decided that it was safer not to even go beyond the second level of communication. But remember that a taciturn partner does not necessarily mean an agreeing one. Buried deeply below many exterior layers may be some very hot coals that were never extinguished. Such a one takes and takes and takes until one day he erupts with volcanic force over an inconsequential matter.

The fifth level of communication is characterized by a limited disclosure of feelings or emotion. "I really wish that we would not go out tonight. I'm just not in the mood."

"Spending that much money on furniture frightens me." At this level real feelings are beginning to emerge.

The sixth level involves real in-depth disclosures about feelings—but only good ones. Some couples may be lulled into a false sense of security by saying, "Of course we can communicate with one another." They then show written notes or recount conversations in which one soul is bared to another. The words would put many poets to shame. It's great! Some never begin to reach this level. The ones who do are fortunate indeed, unless they allow their attainments to prevent their taking the final leap into complete communication.

The seventh level is the crowning glory of communication. Here two people willingly come together with the sole purpose of sharing their deepest feelings on a matter in order that they may jointly reach a satisfactory goal that is agreeable to both. Neither enters such a dialogue with any preconceived ideas of the outcome because it will not become apparent until each can experience the feelings of the other (both good and bad, happy and unhappy) and then make an intelligent decision. It is much like the principle of osmosis in science. Just as two fluids that are separated from each other by a porous membrane pass through the membrane and become one, so do the feelings of two individuals pass into the minds of one another until they become one emotionally. One steps into the shoes of the other. Jointly they see through one another's eyes. The decision that is reached is one of mutual agreement.

The eighth level can only be reached by those who are willing to work their way through the first seven levels. When a husband and wife have mastered the art of fully exposing their feelings to one another in an effort to completely understand how the other one feels so that a mutually satisfactory solution may be reached, then they may convey deepest feelings by a touch or a look without ever speaking a word. Knowing glances and touches are significant on the lower levels of communication, but they are pale in comparison to the coals of a fire that has warmed many winters.

SUGGESTIONS FOR DEVELOPING
GOOD COMMUNICATION

Each case is different and yet there are some principles that have weathered the test of time and should prove useful to most couples.

1. *TRUE COMMUNICATION HAS TO BE A TWO WAY STREET.* Both husband and wife must participate willingly. One mate can explode or tell the other one off, but it takes two to communicate. If one wants to and the other doesn't, the former has a terrific selling responsibility!

2. *REALIZE THAT MEN AND WOMEN ARE USUALLY DIFFERENT IN THEIR EXPRESSIVENESS.* Little boys are generally taught, either directly or by implication, that it is unmanly to show certain emotions, especially the more sensitive and tender ones. "Big boys don't cry." "Men are more concerned with actions than words." Most boys are encouraged to display the emotions connected with aggressiveness but discouraged to show sentimentality. "That's sissy!" Logic and facts appeal to a man. Emotions are paramount to a woman. Men can become more sensitive. Women can learn to handle some matters in a more logical way. Understanding the differences, however, can go far in ameliorating many problems which arise.

3. *GOOD COMMUNICATION IS IMPOSSIBLE WITHOUT TRUST.* Neither party is going to make himself vulnerable to attack very many times. Your mate is not going to tell you how he really feels about something until he first feels secure in expressing himself. Trust has to be earned. We ourselves must be trustworthy of the other's confidences. Slowly but surely, as our mate works his way through the different levels of communication, we offer the security of our

trust. Without fear or reservation, a husband or wife should feel free to admit, "I'm afraid," or "I'm embarrassed," without the worry of being ridiculed or rejected or having the admission thrown up to them at a later time. The need to *be* known and the fear of *being* known constantly battle within each of us. If you have made me feel secure in your love and if I completely trust you, then I am free to place my jumbled thoughts in your hand and feel confident that you will gently blow the chaff away while tenderly grasping the grain.

A young couple just beginning marriage should be aware of how sacred this trust is. It cannot be developed overnight but can come more quickly if both realize its importance and make a conscious effort to make one another feel secure.

4. *BE SENSITIVE TO FEELINGS.* Deep inside each of us is a self-image. It may be called ego, or self-acceptance, or self-esteem, or sense of personal worth. There is nothing selfish about this feeling. In fact, a healthy love of self is a Bible command. In Matthew 22:39 we are told to love our neighbors as ourselves. A person who has a healthy regard for himself will not have to resort to coverups for insecurities. He accepts himself with both strengths and weaknesses.

There is a fundamental truth that should be understood concerning feelings before any effective communication can take place. If the core of a person is attacked, he will come to its defense much as a drowning person will grasp at anything to prevent death. If one partner views communication as a means of attacking the other person, then the victim will only naturally put up a defense. It can follow one of two paths: fight or flight. He can fight by being critical of everyone, by bragging to build himself up, by shouting angry words, by throwing things in a rage. On the other hand, protection of one's self-esteem can follow another course. It can follow the path of flight. Efforts to run away from something that is hurting can take the form of shyness, constantly running oneself down, or even being overly agreeable. But it is only natural to protect one's basic core. A realization of these impulses can go far in paving the way to good communication. Heeding the Golden Rule and treating others as we would wish to be treated is fundamental in being sensitive to the feelings of another.

5. *TAKE TIME FOR COMMUNICATION.* The complete baring of emotions between two people is not going to take place overnight. Sometimes one dials the other but only receives busy signals instead of an answer. The time should be agreeable. Frequently one party is just not in the mood to talk. At other times both may want to talk, but there are just too many irons in the fire. A sizable block of time away from the children and the telephone is needed. The late evening hours provide privacy but frequently husbands and wives are exhausted. Getting away for a night or even a weekend may seem like an extravagance. In reality, however, it is a small price to pay for the development of a healthy marriage.

6. *LEARN THE LANGUAGE OF COMMUNICA-TION.* When two people are trying to get their ideas over to one another, the spoken word is responsible for only seven percent of the meaning that is conveyed. Voice tone accounts for thirty-eight percent, but facial expression and body tone make up fifty-five percent of the impact of the message.

For example, a husband or wife may utter words which, if taken at face value, seem innocent enough. The tone of the voice emits an entirely different message, however. The facial expression and body tone may further intensify negativeness. If a frown is on the face of the one speaking, then even the most courteous words mean nothing.

Words which attack the self-image of the other person should never be used. To say, "You made me mad this morning!" can only stimulate a defence in the hearer. The statement, "I heard some words which upset me today," paves the way for the other person to explain what he meant by those words and thus opens the door of communication.

7. *DEVELOP THE ART OF LISTENING.* Dr. Paul Tournier, an eminent Swiss physician and psychotherapist, speaks of the "dialogues of the deaf, in which no one really listens." When our mate is trying to tell us something, how often do we sit there thinking only of what we ourselves will say as soon as we can get a word in. Instead of interrupting or suggesting, we should learn to sit quietly and absorb every word and every nuance of meaning which the other person is trying to convey. We can learn basic skills in listening, such as looking into only one eye of the person speaking. The listener cannot look attentively into both eyes. Select one (it does not matter whether it is the right one or the left) and look into it steadfastly. Watch your body movements and guard against any action which indicates indifference. Finally, learn to listen to the heart of the speaker and not just the lips.

Of the four basic communication skills (reading, writing, speaking, and listening), we spend the greater part of our time listening and yet have virtually no training in that area. Both at home and at school we are taught how to employ the first three more successfully, but hardly anywhere does anyone find instruction on listening. Forty-six percent of our communication consists of listening, thirty percent is talking, fifteen percent is reading, and nine percent is writing. Is it any wonder communication suffers when we never learn to successfully employ its major component? Most people take listening for granted. "That's easy," they say. "Anybody can listen." However, listening is not only the major part of communication; it is also often the hardest part.

No couple ever learned to listen overnight. The skill cannot be mastered in the midst of a heated argument. Instead, daily, each needs to practice the art of opening up one's ears and truly hearing what the other one has to say. It is best to begin with the small, insignificant matters in order that the skill may be firmly established when weightier matters need to be discussed.

8. *RESOLVE IRRITATIONS BEFORE THEY CAN FESTER.* Good communication avoids outbursts. Ephesians 4:26,27 admonishes Christians: "Be ye angry, and sin not: let not the sun go down upon your wrath." Anger, or a normal irritation of emotions, is inevitable as two people live together. There is no reason for anger to become rage, however, if it is resolved on a regular basis before it festers and gets out of control. Anger should never be allowed to smolder only to burst into flames later. Its devastating effects can be neutralized by dealing with them as soon as possible. Some irritations fade into insignificance after only a few hours and can be dismissed, so it is frequently best to learn to allow a little cooling off time. Nevertheless, if something is really bothering either husband or wife, no matter how trivial it may seem to the other, the wise couple—very early in the marriage—will learn to discuss and resolve these points of irritation before they can become major problems.

9. *REALIZE THAT COMMUNICATION IS INTENDED FOR GROWTH THROUGH PROBLEM SOLVING INSTEAD OF TEARING THE OTHER PERSON DOWN.* So many have a negative concept of communication and view it erroneously as a method of *telling the other person off.* Nothing is achieved through this concept. Only defensive anger and resentment can result. Instead of getting even with the

offender, communication should be viewed in a positive light as a means of working through daily problems. So many times one mate has no idea that a problem even exists. Certainly no solution can be reached until it is brought out into the open through communication.

10. *EXCEPT IN MATTERS OF RIGHT OR WRONG, COMMUNICATION IS FOR THE PURPOSE OF CHANGE WHEN A PROBLEM EXISTS. BOTH PARTIES SHOULD BE WILLING TO SHIFT TOWARD COMMON GROUND.* For example, suppose the problem happens to be a lack of money in the household. Both should be willing to trim their spending. She may agree to cut down on her shopping sprees and he may reduce his spending on a hobby. Or she could better control impulse buying for the house and he could be more conservative in his selection of a new car. Whatever the problem, it is unfair for one to be expected to do all the changing. Both must be willing to make some adjustments.

11. *COUPLES SHOULD FIRST LEARN TO TALK HONESTLY IN NONTHREATENING AREAS BEFORE THEY CAN EVEN ATTEMPT TO EXPLORE ONE ANOTHER'S FEELINGS ON SUCH SUBJECTS AS FEARS, INSECURITIES, JEALOUSY, A NEW JOB, OR MOVING TO A NEW LOCATION.* They should practice expressing themselves on such subjects as favorite people, preferences in books, or opinions on current happenings. A few openers might be:

   (1) Your greatest joy
   (2) The most influential person in your childhood
   (3) A time when you genuinely wished that you could have gone through the floor
   (4) The nicest compliment you ever received
   (5) Your favorite color and the reason

(6) The person most respected by you in your adult world of today, outside of your family

(7) Your greatest apprehension about growing older

(8) Your feelings about suffering and pain

Remember that it is exceedingly difficult for some people to express themselves. It may be a matter of genes and chromosomes or an early nonexpressive environment (or a combination of the two). If your mate was reared in a household in which no one ever probed below the factual level of conversation, do not expect a soul-searching talk the week after marriage.

Every couple should remember that most men, by nature, are more reticent than women. Up to this point their whole world discouraged a display of feelings. It will require love, patience, and kindness for a man to openly communicate his feelings. The wife may have to take the initiative in creating an atmosphere of love and trust. The more one partner asks the other to talk, the more silent he becomes.

Sometimes people can write their feelings better than they can express them orally. It may be easier to select a noncontroversial subject and have each one go into a separate room and write on that line of thought for about thirty minutes. Then they can exchange papers and read what the other person thinks about that particular matter. It may not be ideal, but at least it is a beginning.

12. *NO ONE HAS THE RIGHT TO ATTACH MOTIVES TO WHAT ANOTHER PERSON SAYS OR DOES.* However, he can accurately report what he perceives by touch, sight, or sound. For example, "You never took your eyes off the TV when I was trying to talk to you," is a statement of fact. You may add, "I thought you probably were not interested in what I had to say." That was your perception of what

you saw. However, only the other person can accurately relate what his true feelings were because only he knows. He could say something such as, "Honey, I was very interested in what you were saying and had been following your line of thought very closely. It is just that this was a crucial play in the most important game of the season." It is hard to compete against an act such as that! You saw his rapt attention to the television and had every right to report what your feelings were, but you had no right to surmise what the other person intended. When you say, "I saw the frown on your face and thought perhaps you were angry with me," you are accurately relating what you saw with your eyes and also your perception of what you saw. But you have no right to say what the other person intended by that frown. It could have been heartburn, and he is the only one who can tell what his intentions were.

We may accurately say what our ears hear. "I heard you say that you did not want to go." Or "I heard the lack of enthusiasm in your voice." Both statements describe what you heard with your ears, but only the other person has the right to say what he intended. "You drew away when I touched you," allows the other person to know what you felt by touch; but only he can tell you his reasons for drawing away.

It is all right to kindly report what you heard, saw, or learned by the sense of touch; but you have no right to attach motives to the other person's actions.

13. *THE BASIC ELEMENT UNDERLYING ALL COMMUNICATION IS LOVE.* In its deepest sense, communication is the baring of one soul to another. Behind the facade of the problems and issues, two people are crying to each other, "Look at the real me living down here. I have feelings. I hurt. Please try to step into my shoes and see through my eyes." No

person in his right mind is going to thus expose himself until he feels secure in that relationship. The thirteenth chapter of 1 Corinthians gives the characteristics of such love. True love is patient, kind, generous, humble, unselfish, not angered easily, not suspicious, looks for the good instead of the evil, and lasts through all circumstances. To try to have good communication without the proper love is impossible.

Perhaps we are trying to get the cart before the horse.

SUMMARY

Good communication is an in-depth sharing of feelings between two people in an effort to search for a solution to a problem.

These suggestions make communication easier from the beginning:

1. Good communication has to be a two way street.

2. Realize that men and women are usually different in their expressiveness.

3. Good communication is impossible without trust.

4. Be sensitive to feelings.

5. Take time.

6. Learn the language.

7. Develop the art of listening.

8. Resolve irritations before they can fester.

9. Realize that communication is intended for growth through problem solving, not tearing the other person down.

10. Except in matters of right or wrong, communication is for the purpose of change when a problem exists. Both

parties should be willing to shift toward common ground.

11. Couples should first learn to talk honestly in nonthreatening areas.

12. No one has the right to attach motives to what another person says or does.

13. The basic element underlying all communication is love.

SUGGESTIONS FOR CLASS DISCUSSION
Chapter 4

1. What is the life blood of any joint endeavor? Apply this principle to government, industry, school, sports, and church. Why is it so essential in marriage?

2. In Ephesians 5:21-31 Paul compared the relationship between husband and wife to what other relationship? Discuss the depth of the two types of love.

3. State the definition of true communication as it was set forth in this chapter. Do you agree or disagree?

4. Compare a lack of communication to a crack in the foundation of marriage. What happens to that crack as more and more pressure is placed upon it?

5. The first level of communication is chitchat. Cite some examples. Is there anything wrong with this level?

6. What is the second level of communication? What are its values?

7. The third level of communication is called testing the water. How does it protect us from risk? Is this bad?

8. The fourth level involves lightly risking one's ideas and judgments. What usually happens to a shy person if his or her ideas are not accepted? Does silence necessarily imply agreement?

9. What is the fifth level of communication? Give some examples.

10. The sixth level involves real in-depth disclosures about feelings. Which feelings are expressed? What are the dangers?

11. Why is the seventh level termed the crowning glory of communication? Why can there be no preconceived ideas of the outcome?

12. The eighth level of communication, expressed simply by a touch or a glance, can only be achieved to the fullest extent when two people have worked their way through the other seven levels. Why is it dangerous to rely upon this method until complete understanding has been achieved?

13. The lesson stated that communication has to be a two way street. Can only one partner communicate? Why?

14. How do men and women differ in their abilities to express themselves?

15. Do you agree or disagree with the statement that good communication is impossible without trust? Why?

16. If the core of a person (self-image or ego) is attacked, what is the natural reaction? What does this principle teach us regarding the manner with which we treat our mates?

17. Good communication requires time. Make some suggestions for finding the necessary time.

18. Why are facial expressions and voice tone more important than the actual words uttered in communicating with one another?

19. Why is it better to say, "I heard some words which upset me today," rather than "You made me mad this morning!"?

20. Discuss some of the suggested skills to be developed in the art of listening.

21. According to Ephesians 4:26,27, when should anger be settled? What are some of the dangers of unresolved anger?

22. How can good communication be an avenue for growth through problem solving? Should it ever be used to tear the other person down?

23. Using a lack of money as an example, explain how both husband and wife can shift toward a common ground.

24. How can couples learn to talk honestly in nonthreatening areas? Use specific examples.

25. Explain the difference in accurately reporting what you see or hear and in attaching motives to what the other person says or does.

26. What is the basic element underlying all communication?

EXERCISES

Exercise 1

Both partners should individually answer the following questions by marking each as either true or false.

_____ 1. I am satisfied with the way my partner shares feelings.

_____ 2. I would say that my partner is usually a good listener.

_____ 3. I find it easy to tell my partner my true feelings.

_____ 4. I am not afraid to request of my partner what I truly want.

_____ 5. My partner and I talk to each other satisfactorily.

_____ 6. I seldom get the silent treatment from my partner when there is a problem that needs to be discussed.

_____ 7. I have no difficulty believing everything my partner tells me.

_____ 8. I usually share negative feelings about my partner, knowing that neither of us will become angry.

_____ 9. My partner is fair and objective and does not make comments that put me down.

_____ 10. I do not assume that my partner knows my feelings.

The value of each true answer is ten points. What is your total score? Work on each statement answered false. If the total score is less than 70 points, work on your whole marriage!

Exercise 2
Complete the following statements individually and then compare notes with your mate.

1. What I like most about you is _____.

2. In our marriage I feel close to you when _____.

3. I am most fearful in our marriage when _____.

4. I am angriest with our relationship when _____.

5. I feel loved in our relationship when you _____.

6. The feelings I find hardest to share with you are _____.

7. In our marriage I would like more _____.

8. As your mate I feel uneasy when _____.

9. As your spouse I feel distance between us when _____.

10. In our partnership I would like less _____.

11. As your spouse I feel appreciated when _____.

12. The one thing in our relationship that needs the most attention now is _____.

I DO!

5

Commitment has become the latest "dirty" word to be added to our mother tongue. It is vital to any really successful venture. Athletic coaches call for it (then you hear about illegal money, cars, narcotics, sexual favors, etc., ad nauseam); the military demands it (and we hear of more and more spying and turning over classified documents to the enemy); politicians talk about it (and we see corruption, lying, mudslinging campaigning, pork barrel legislation, and nepotism); preachers preach about it (and confess, when caught, to "indiscretions," misappropriation of funds, less-than-honorable fund raising techniques, etc.); churches demand it (and have large congregations of adulterers openly living with second, third, or fourth "spouses"; financing illegal operations; making whiskey; running casinos; condoning homosexuality—you name it and it can be found somewhere). Where has commitment gone? It's like looking for a needle in a haystack to try to find it.

Today there are three divorces for every four marriages. What is the missing ingredient? Commitment. It is one of the two ingredients that form that marvelous *super glue* called love. Without commitment it becomes more like a poor quality cellophane tape. A nice name for commitment is *integrity*. Job was said to be a man of integrity (Job 2:3). In all his troubles he would neither sin nor charge God foolishly (Job 1:22). Good character and integrity go hand in hand. It is impossible for people without character to have any integrity.

SHE IS MY EVERYTHING

A wedding day is a great day! Preceding it have been the days of dating and courtship, the engagement, the long round of social events, all the planning and shopping. The day itself is filled with hectic activity. All these are a part of the culture in which we live. The wedding itself is a beautiful display of flowers, candles, music, and dress. Friends come from far and near to witness the ceremony and to share the joy of the day in the reception following. It is all such a breathtaking whirlwind of activities that often the bride and groom are almost in a state of shock. Beyond the glitter and glimmer of the moment and the pictures that enable them to recall the events of the day, do they really comprehend what they have done?

Mixed in with songs and messages and prayers is the exchange of solemn vows: "Do you take this woman as your lawfully wedded wife? Do you promise to live together after God's ordinances? Do you promise to love, honor, and cherish her in sickness and in health, in adversity and in prosperity, for better or for worse until you are parted by death?" Those are big promises and *until death* means through the entire lifetime of one and perhaps both. Is it possible that we have allowed the glamour of the occasion to overshadow the real meaning? The other things are all nice but you can have a marriage without them. These vows, though, are not just a part of everything else that is happening; they *are* what is happening—the whole thing. Without them there is no marriage. With marriage being the most serious of all earthly covenants, isn't it about time that we give these vows the important place they deserve?

Marriage is a covenant that promises a lifelong commitment. The very word *commitment* has almost become a joke in today's laid-back society. What is it? It is the desire to succeed; the determination to succeed; the willingness to pay the price to succeed. In short it's integrity. In down-to-earth language, it's guts. It requires grit in the gizzard and sanctified stubbornness. Though marriage itself should never be a battlefield, there are many things that have to be fought in order to hold it together. One young man telegraphed his father about a fight he had won back during the days of "fight until one drops," saying, "Won easily in 85 rounds." There is a lot of that kind of stamina needed in marriage. That's commitment. It is necessary to any long-term endeavor, and there is nothing more long-term than "until we are parted by death." Ask a young man about success in a major sport and he will tell you what commitment is. Ask a young woman about success in higher education in some difficult field and she will tell you what commitment is. Is it unreasonable to ask a bride and groom and expect them to know what commitment is?

The state recognizes marriage as a binding contract and attaches stiff penalties in the event it is broken. The reason is we live in a country whose laws are based on Bible principles. God recognizes marriage as a binding contract. In Matthew 19:1-9 Jesus spelled it out in no uncertain terms. The state requires blood tests, a license, a ceremony, and signatures. God requires commitment.

While it is true that commitment requires guts, it also requires love. Like the super glue that requires the mixing of two ingredients in order to achieve the super bonding it is known for, commitment requires the mixing of love and integrity to give it its lasting quality. Often the thing that is glued together will itself break before the glue will. In the same way, life itself will end before the real love and integrity that bind the partners together in marriage will give way. In Ephesians 5:25 husbands are commanded to love their wives like Christ loved the church. In Titus 2:4 the older women are to teach the younger women to love their husbands. The love of courtship days and early years of marriage is electrifying. Hormones are poured into the bloodstream by the gallons—bells ring, lights flash. It is an exciting time in life. As love matures it does not lose this excitement but it does harness it to greater service. In examining the characteristics of love in 1 Corinthians 13 you see how love mixed with integrity makes an unbreakable union. Paul says, "Love . . .

SUFFERS LONG—'I'll be patient with you. I'm human, too.'

IS KIND—'I'll treat you like I want you to treat me.'

ENVIES NOT—'There is absolutely no jealousy in me.'

~ *VAUNTS NOT ITSELF*—'I understand that we are different but I also understand that we are equals.'

IS NOT PUFFED UP—'I promise not to let my little successes go to my head.'

DOES NOT BEHAVE ITSELF UNSEEMLY—'I will always treat you with honor and respect.'

SEEKS NOT HER OWN—'I want to do what is best for you.'

IS NOT EASILY PROVOKED—'I take into account that we all have bad days.'

THINKS NO EVIL—'I trust you completely.'

REJOICES NOT IN INIQUITY—'I'm sorry about the mistakes I've made.'

BEARS ALL THINGS—'The loads of life are heavy but I'll always bear my fair share.'

HOPES ALL THINGS—'I'll never let our dreams die.'

ENDURES ALL THINGS—'I love you with a tough love. It's not a *because* love or an *if* love; it's unconditional.'"

Is it any wonder that the conclusion drawn is, "Love never fails"? The super glue of commitment will never fail where love and integrity are the two key ingredients. If marriage is held together by something as flimsy as chewing gum, we will spit it out as soon as it loses its flavor. When God said, "Therefore shall a man leave his father and his mother, and shall cleave unto his wife: and they shall be one flesh" (Genesis 2:24), I think it is significant that the Hebrew word chosen for *cleave* is also the word for *glue*. It's a strong word. There is no hint of chewing gum here.

In view of the lifetime and eternal consequences of this great commitment, much more teaching needs to be done in the home, in the church, and in pre-marriage counseling sessions. Once you have made the vows you have reached *the point of no return.* When a plane departs a west coast airport and heads out across the vast expanse of the Pacific Ocean toward a destination in the Far East, it reaches a point where there is no turning back. Before that point is reached, it has enough fuel to turn back to the point of origin. Beyond that point there is no alternative; it must continue toward its destination. It's called "the point of no return." When a space shuttle is launched from Cape Kennedy, there is an opportunity, up to a given point, to turn back and land there. Beyond that point there is no turning back. Its next alternative is to land in West Africa. It has reached *the point of no return.* Many marriages should never take place. Before the vows are made the marriage should be called off. But for all marriages, once the vows are made, they have passed *the point of no return.* Why do so few understand this solemn truth?

Marriage is undertaken voluntarily. "Do you take this man or woman?" You have the option at that point. Five years later or twenty-five years later you still take them because of the commitment of those vows. "Do you take as your lawfully wedded" wife or husband? After the vows neither party has the right to say, "What business of yours is it if I do such and such?" It's your business because you are partners in life as long as you both are alive. "Do you promise to live together after God's ordinances?" You vow to keep God's laws concerning marriage. Do you know what those laws are? Do you review them periodically to make sure you still know? Baptism is more than an immersion and marriage is more than a ceremony. When marriage is built upon God's ordinances and people enter this holy union without even knowing these ordinances, how can we expect the marriage to last?

The wife of a man in the town where we live suffered from steadily and rapidly declining health. Most of the things a man expects from his wife she could not give him. Because there were others who could care for her, she begged him to find someone else who could be a better wife to him. For him the idea was unthinkable. He cared for her tenderly, bathed her, fed her, helped care for all her bodily functions. Finally she lost even the use of her mind and the time came when he could no longer care for her by himself. He placed her in a nursing home where he visits her every day and spends most of the day with her. He still feeds her, talks to her, bathes her. Some asked, "Why? She doesn't even know you are here." His answer: "It's a matter of love and integrity. Because I love her I made a commitment to her for as long as she lives. I intend to honor that commitment. I still love her and she is still my wife. True, she may not know I am here but I know I'm here and that's important to me." That's what you mean when you say, "I do."

Several years ago when I was in my early twenties and my father-in-law was in his mid-fifties, he started to pick up a heavy box. I stepped in and said, "Let me do that." His natural reply was "Why?" "Because I'm young and strong," I said. Proceeding to pick up the box, he reminded me, "Well, I'm old and tough." The commitment of marriage is for the young and strong *and* for the old and tough.

HE IS MY ALL

I have never noticed a little boy pretending he is getting married. It is a favorite pastime with little girls. Watch them play dress-up. Any cast off dress can become a vision of loveliness as they float down the aisle.

Ask a teenage boy what he wants to do when he grows up. His aspirations normally center around a job, a career, and their material benefits. A teenage girl, on the other hand, may pinpoint a specific career but such a choice is usually based upon the foundation of a home.

Listen to the conversation of a group of men. It centers around their jobs, some sporting event, or a happening in the news. If several women are thrown together long enough, some aspect of the home will inevitably creep in whether it pertains to rearing children, something new for the house, or a favorite recipe.

A longing for a home is an integral part of my being as a woman. My husband holds the key to my security. I desperately need his commitment that he is dedicated to joining hands with me in making this marriage work.

Few brides—or grooms—have any idea of the depth of commitment in the marriage vows. I didn't. If it were not for the recording, I would not even remember the words themselves. A bride and groom will usually make the same promises to one another, yet their commitments are inevitably colored by different hues. As a woman I need the security of your promises in the following areas.

1. *MATERIAL POSSESSIONS*—I am not speaking of the elaborate glittering frills of life but rather the basic needs. In spite of all the propaganda concerning the newer role of women in the world, I really do not want the burden of providing a living for a family thrust upon my shoulders. I long for the protecting arms of my husband in this respect. Please take your position as provider seriously and be responsible. Do not make me wonder where I will find money to buy the groceries or shoes for the children. I am aware of the importance of my role in managing.

2. *SEXUAL FIDELITY*—I have given every fiber of my body to you sexually. In return I deserve your complete faithfulness. For centuries there has been a double standard in marriage regarding physical unfaithfulness. Now the gap has narrowed as the present woman of the world demands equality in every phase of life—even promiscuity. A Christian husband and wife, however, should never give Satan an opportunity for temptation. Our commitment to one another has the inherent understanding that neither one of us will ever allow ourselves to be placed in a situation in which marital infidelity could ever develop.

3. *EMOTIONAL SUPPORT*—I not only should be assured that you will never even entertain the idea of

sexual unfaithfulness but I also desperately need to know that you will never leave me emotionally. Pulling together we can face almost any situation. Since the basic longing for a happy home is such an integral part of my makeup, please do not attack the very foundation of my being by pulling away from me emotionally. I realize that many factors can build a defensive shield around either of us, but please join hands with me in working through our problems to prevent any emotional conflict. Perhaps more than you, I deeply crave the security of knowing that you will always be by my side.

4. *SPIRITUAL LEADERSHIP*—Into your hands has been placed the leadership of the home (Ephesians 5:22-33), including spiritual matters. Many women, however, face the prospect not only of serving God alone but also the realization that the salvation of the children's souls rests primarily upon the mother's shoulders.

Ideally we lean upon one another. Sometimes I become discouraged spiritually and look to you for the strength to get me through my valleys. There are other times when I realize that you are in a spiritual holding pattern and seek inspiration from me. Together we balance one another.

Since God in His master plan has entrusted the spiritual guidance of the home into your hands, please do not disappoint me. Set the way for me and our children. Fathers are divinely instructed to bring their children up in the nurture and admonition of the Lord (Ephesians 6:4). As a mother, I want to draw my children close and tell them the rich stories from God's Word but I also need your support. Our children must have your example as well as your direct instruction.

5. *OLD AGE*—Very seldom do a young bride and groom seriously consider the implications of their vows in their golden years at the time those promises are made. Nearly everyone wishfully believes that old age is the

lot of someone else. It is difficult for the bride to even imagine her handsome groom as stooped or gray. The young husband sees only a vision of loveliness. A wrinkled old woman? Perhaps confined to her bed for the rest of her life? Never! Things such as that happen to other people.

But husbands and wives do grow older. Their appearances change. Health will progressively fail if they live long enough. An accident or some other stroke of misfortune can alter the entire course of two young lives. Both husbands and wives need the assurance that they will never be forsaken. It seems that the woman feels more vulnerable than the man does in this respect and needs the assurance of his commitment. Both need to plan for reality and prepare materially for later years. Together they can face almost any adversity, provided they include God as their partner.

I remember a time a number of years ago when my Don slept on the cold tile floor of an intensive care room in the hospital so he could be near me. How indelibly stamped upon my mind are the months of convalescence when he so lovingly cared for my every need and so gently guided me back into a useful life. As difficult as that time was earlier in our marriage, it is comforting to know that he will always be there. That is commitment!

SUMMING IT UP

1. Commitment has become a joke, perhaps even a *dirty* word, in today's society.

2. "Till we are parted by death" is a solemn vow that demands something special to make it endure.

3. When mixed together, love and integrity make a "super glue."

4. The exchange of marriage vows puts a couple at the *point of no return.*

5. This life of marriage must be lived "after the ordinances of God." Do you know what those ordinances are ?

6. Though men and women are completely different creatures, the basic needs of both are fulfilled in the commitment of marriage.

SUGGESTIONS FOR CLASS DISCUSSION
Chapter 5

1. In a brain-storming session have each class member write a synonym for *commitment.* Compare the results.

2. In what way did Job prove his commitment or integrity?

3. What sort of commitment to the marriage relationship did God outline in Matthew 19:1-9?

4. Marriage requires the blending of what two ingredients? Describe a union characterized by only one of these.

5. In the fifth chapter of Ephesians husbands are commanded to love their wives as Christ loved the church. Discuss the results of Christ's love for the church.

6. Contrast the love of courtship days with mature love. Is either better than the other?

7. Assign each class member one of the characteristics of love as mentioned in 1 Corinthians 13. Discuss the results.

8. In Genesis 2:24 the Hebrew word for *cleave* is also the word for *glue.* Discuss the implications.

9. Where is *the point of no return* in marriage?

10. What is the meaning of commitment when one party must spend years in a nursing home or in some other way be incapacitated?

11. How do men and women usually differ in the importance which each places on the home in their lives?

12. How does a woman feel about her husband's commitment in the realm of material possessions? Can you detect a change in this area over the past 50 years?

13. God gave sexual infidelity as the only valid reason for breaking the marriage contract and entering into another union (Matthew 19). Why is commitment in this realm of the relationship so important?

14. Why is commitment to the emotional needs of one another so vital?

15. Into whose hands has God placed the spiritual leadership of the home? What are the implications?

16. How does commitment in old age differ from that of the first few years of marriage? Is it any less intense?

(See next page for exercise)

EXERCISE

One of the best ways to measure commitment is the amount of time which we normally devote to that person, possession, event, or cause. How much real time do you devote to your marriage each week? Talking about what you will have for dinner, errands that need to be run, bills that need to be paid, or the children's grades will not count. It must be time alone without any distractions such as television, phone calls, or newspapers. Select your best time and set aside ten or fifteen minutes each day to talk about your feelings, your frustrations, your sorrows, your happiness—anything which pertains to the real you. Keep a record of the time until this activity becomes a habit.

	Time
Sunday	_____
Monday	_____
Tuesday	_____
Wednesday	_____
Thursday	_____
Friday	_____
Saturday	_____

HOW TO LEAD
BY FOLLOWING

6

We live in a world today that has made an all-out assault on marriage. One campaign of that war has been conducted against the traditional Bible roles within the family. Satan is advocating anarchy within the home and just a glance around us shows that he is achieving some success. With the talk about role reversal ("house husbands") and even sex change operations, is it any wonder that a generation growing up doesn't really know which way to turn?

Most of the problem arises from selfishness and from ignorance of what submission really is. In this lawless world nobody wants to submit to anybody. It appears to be a manifestation of weakness and carries with it the idea of groveling. The answer? Everybody be a chief! All the books about self-assertiveness, having your own way, and learning the art of intimidation reflect that mentality. Is the Bible teaching on submission really that distasteful? Not at all. In reality it is simply being Christ-like; in other words it is being a Christian. That affects every relationship of life including marriage.

Much has been made of the fact that wives are told in the Bible to submit to their husbands (Ephesians 5:22). In fact it is often treated as if this were the only thing the Bible says on the subject. In stressing the woman's responsibility in this matter, it is often overlooked that the preceding verse says, "Submitting yourselves one to another in the fear of God." These words are addressed to all Christians. Then the principle of mutual submission is applied to many different relationships. It just happens that the first of these is marriage. When a man and a woman vow their lifetime commitment to each other, they also enter a relationship that demands a lifetime of submission to one another.

Philippians chapter two admonishes us to have the mind of Christ and then develops the theme of Christ's submission. Having the mind of Christ (which every Christian must have) produces mutual submission. It was Jesus' submission to the will of the Father that carried Him to and held Him on the cross (Philippians 2:5-8). He was not there because He was inferior, but because He chose through love to submit to His Father. He said, "I came down from heaven, not to do mine own will, but the will of him that sent me" (John 6:38).

Because roles are different, why must so many assume they are adversaries? The roles of Jesus the Son and God the Father are different, but they are not adversary roles. Jesus was in every way equal to the Father. He said, "I and my father are one" (John 10:30). In Philippians 2:6 Paul said Jesus was equal to God yet He counted that not a thing to be selfishly grasped. His submission to the Father was an action of love.

The roles of male and female are different. Those roles were made different from the beginning. Man and woman were created for different roles. God made woman to be a helper *suitable* for her husband (Genesis 2:18). The word translated *suitable* means *counterpart*. Woman is simply an equal of a different kind. Galatians 3:26-28 says this equality of different roles is true of Christianity. Neither in the home nor in the church are the differing roles to be adversary roles.

The necessity of different roles grows out of the variations of work to be accomplished and from the all-pervasive need of orderliness (1 Corinthians 14:40). In every worthwhile endeavor there must be well-defined roles. What physical endeavor is more worthwhile than marriage and the home it creates? How can two so diverse as male and female (with the added diversity of the individual personality of each) function so efficiently that they can actually be called *one flesh*? The answer is given in the Bible, and when the Bible is followed marriage works beautifully. If man and woman, husband and wife, are truly equal, why is the husband designated as head? God Himself mentions three reasons: the order of creation, man being first; the order of sin, woman being first; and the nature of sin, woman being beguiled by subtlety. But, after all, someone must be responsible. Do you remember the crash of Eastern flight 401 in the Florida Everglades several years age? That L1011 had a malfunctioning light on one of the flight instrument panels. First one, then another tried to fix it. Even the pilots became engrossed with the little light. The plane crashed because nobody was flying it. In marriage somebody must *fly the plane*. God designated the husband as the pilot.

In the church elders lead and rule the congregation (Acts 20:28). Yet Peter warns them against lording over the spiritual family (1 Peter 5:3). The roles are different and yet there is equality and no sense of being adversaries. The roles of men and women in the church are different. Both are teachers (2 Timothy 2:2). The word translated *men* is the generic word *anthropos* meaning mankind (both male and female), but roles differ. Woman is forbidden to teach over or usurp authority over men (1 Timothy 2:11,12). Though the roles differ, there is absolute equality and neither is to view the other as an adversary.

In the long discussion about the diversity of spiritual gifts in the first century church, it was made quite clear that, though many different roles were assigned, no gift was superior and no conflict was to exist in that great diversity. Each needed the other in order to be complete. By each observing his assigned role there would be no confusion; peace would reign (1 Corinthians 14:33).

AM I A MAN OR A MOUSE?

The Bible teaches that the husband is the head of the wife. To the Corinthians Paul wrote, "But I would have you know, that . . . the head of the woman is the man" (1 Corinthians 11:3). To the Ephesians he wrote, "For the husband is the head of the wife . . ." (Ephesians 5:23). This latter statement is separated by only one verse from the statement, "Submitting yourselves one to another . . ." (verse 21). What does this mean? It means that the husband is to provide the meaningful, responsible leadership the home requires without being dictatorial and ignoring the wisdom and talent of his wife. Remember, she is to guide and keep the home (1 Timothy 5:14; Titus 2:4). They are partners in a joint venture that requires the best they both have to offer.

The Bible says several things about a husband's role of leadership in the home.

1. It is to be provided in love (Ephesians 5:25; Colossians 3:19).

2. This love is to equal his love for his own life (Ephesians 5:28).

3. It is to be patterned after Christ's love for the church (Ephesians 5:28).

4. It is to be provided free of bitterness (Colossians 3:19).

5. It is to be done with understanding (1 Peter 3:7).

6. It is to be done in full recognition of the equality of his wife in the sight of God (1 Peter 3:7).

Specifically what do I owe my wife in my role of leadership?

1. I am to love and cherish her (Ephesians 5:28,29).

2. I am to honor her (1 Peter 3:7).

3. I am to take the time necessary to really know her (1 Peter 3:7).

4. I am to protect her from all things that would harm or hurt her (1 Peter 3:7).

5. I am to be the provider for all her needs (1 Timothy 5:8). Though physical needs are specifically under consideration, the underlying principle is broad enough to include all her needs.

6. I am to provide spiritual leadership (Ephesians 5:23).

7. I am to treat her as an equal (1 Peter 3:7; 1 Timothy 5:14; Titus 2:4). I respect her good judgment and talent.

8. I am to make her queen of my life and my home (1 Timothy 5:14; Titus 2:4).

9. I am to honor her above my mother and father (Matthew 19:5).

10. I am to make her my one and only wife as long as she lives (Matthew 19:6).

QUEEN OR SLAVE
WHICH AM I?

Please bear with us as women in our confusion. We are caught up in the center of a conflict. Nearly every magazine which we read bombards us with self-assertiveness and the rights of women. We are told to stand up for ourselves and refuse to tolerate unfair treatment from anyone. On the other hand, from the pulpit we hear lessons from a man with such words as "thy desire shall be to thy husband and he shall rule over thee . . . obedient to their own husbands . . . submit yourselves unto your own husbands . . . be in subjection to your own husbands" (even unbelievers). As Christians, we sincerely want to be whatever God wills and be saved eternally; but no person, male or female, wants to serve as a slave obeying every whim and wish of a ruling monarch. We hear Ephesians 5:22 quoted often: "Wives, submit yourselves unto your own husbands, as unto the Lord," but there seems to be a paucity of lessons on the husband's responsibilities as outlined in the same chapter. Ladies' classes discuss ways to be good wives, but men rarely study lessons on becoming better husbands. Quite frankly, the majority of Christian women regard subjection as bad-tasting medicine that is necessary for salvation but bitter to swallow. Most resent the apparent unconcern of their husbands in learning what role they themselves are to play.

Personally, as a young bride, I accepted my role of submission with the same faith which prompted my obedience to the command: "He that believeth and is baptized shall be saved." It never entered my mind to do otherwise. I willingly accepted Don as my protector and I became his cherished one. We entered this matter of fulfilling the proper roles from the beginning. To be truthful, I have never encountered the problems which many have related to me as I have traveled across the country. A surprising number of God-fearing women are virtual slaves within their own homes. On the other hand, I have had so many radiant women tell me that they have accepted the scriptures concerning roles and have been treated as queens. Their smiles confirm the fact that God's plan does work.

Ephesians 5:32 speaks of the "great mystery." This mystery alludes not only to the relationship of Christ and the church but also to the husband and wife union, both emotionally and physically.

If I try to reform my husband and change his ways, I have met head-on with a brick wall. My assertiveness will not cause him to budge an inch. In fact he will automatically protect himself with a defensive shield. His wounded ego may retreat to the cave of silence or charge on the battlefield of rage.

Within my hands I have a powerful tool at my disposal.

The only manner by which I can change my husband is to change my own attitude. This principle is known as behavior modification. The actions of others are automatic reflexes of the way I treat them. Walk down the street and smile at a stranger. Ninety-nine times out of a hundred he or she will smile in return. A frown elicits a scowl from the other person. When I willingly accept my husband as my protector, something mysterious happens to him. No longer does he consider me as inferior or even equal. I have now been placed on a pedestal. I am his queen. My role of willing submission meets one of his most important needs: to be respected and regarded as the protector of the family (Ephesians 5:29). It stimulates a wonderful response in the male ego. It is one of tender and caring concern. No person ever mistreats someone or something which he or she cherishes. My submission mysteriously evokes a loving, protective emotion. The key to the fifth chapter of Ephesians lies in verse 22: " . . . as unto the Lord." By faith, I joyfully submit to his protection just as lovingly as I accept the encircling arms of Christ as my Lord. I am a complete circle within another circle. My husband and I are distinct individuals. There is some space between us. However, within the loving, protective arms of another I am free to develop my own potentialities to the fullest. I can blossom as one of God's loveliest handiworks. The world can be a frightening arena. If I try to battle singlehandedly, the only way I can survive is to become hardened much as bare feet develop tough protective skin to shield them from the rocks in the road. A pearl is the result of an oyster's attempt to defend itself against an irritation, but somehow a woman who has become hardened by one protective layer after another is not quite as beautiful nor as priceless as a pearl.

If a woman is to reap the greatest joys from her role of submission, there is a prerequisite. She must have a good self-image. If she does not have a high opinion of herself, she will inevitably regard the situation as one of servitude. I must be able to say, "I am a person of worth who has chosen to place myself under the loving, cherishing care of my husband." I do not bring a glass of water upon the command of a lord, but I cannot do enough for one who loves me dearly.

Some readers may be skeptical, but let me pass on this word of advice. *Don't knock it until you've tried it.* It's rather nice to be dragged to the ladies' clothing section of a store and there be instructed to try on clothes "to see if there's not something very special you'd like to have." It is not too terribly degrading to stand back and allow your husband to open doors and pull out chairs for you. I can tolerate the little surprises that repeatedly appear under a pillow, on the kitchen table, or in the closet. I may fuss a bit, but I really do not mind the money he slips into my dresser drawer with the firm instruction: "This is just for you to spend for anything you wish." I think I can tolerate his wanting to take me on a special trip for our anniversary. I can even withstand the rather firm words, "Let me fix breakfast. I really want to!"

I have had women tell me, "I would willingly accept my role of submission if my husband would treat me like that." But we do not submit *if*. We submit *because*—because God said that is the best and the only way. The benefits follow our acceptance.

Esau sold his birthright for a mess of pottage. I'm not about to sell my place as queen in my husband's life for any equal rights movement. The modern woman may have come a long way but I have been at the summit for many years. I'll take the role of submission any day!

WHAT WE HAVE LEARNED

1. The roles in marriage are God-given.

2. Submission is a beautiful attitude that is not confined to a role.

3. "Henpecked" husbands and "enslaved" wives violate both the law of roles and the principle of submission.

4. Roles in marriage, as in all other institutions, must be complimentary and not adversary in nature.

5. The responsibility of leadership gives no one in that role the right to "lord it over" others.

6. A proper understanding of roles and submission enables us to grasp that wonderful equality we hold in God's plan.

SUGGESTIONS FOR CLASS DISCUSSION
Chapter 6

1. Before class assign several members the task of collecting newspaper and magazine articles depicting the war against the traditional roles of the family. Discuss the findings.

2. What are the two major causes of this condition?

3. Ephesians 5:22 is often quoted in sermons and Bible lessons. Notice verse 21. What does the phrase *submitting to one another* mean?

4. Nails did not hold Jesus to the cross. Discuss Philippians 2:5-8 to discover the real reason and power that did hold Him.

5. Christ came to do the "will of him that sent me" (John 6:38). Was He inferior to the Father? How could Christ be in submission and yet utter: "I and my father are one" (John 10:30)?

6. According to Genesis 2:18, what was woman's role? How can she be an equal of a different kind?

7. Orderliness is commanded in 1 Corinthians 14:40. Cite examples of the necessity of this principle in everyday situations.

8. If husband and wife are truly equal, why is the husband designated as the head?

9. Elders are commanded to lead and rule the congregation (Acts 20:28). What is the difference in this role and that of lording it over the spiritual family (1 Peter 5:3)?

10. What is the difference in the roles of men and women in the church? Why?

11. In the first century church why was there a diversity of spiritual gifts (1 Corinthians 14)?

12. Discuss the statement: "The husband is to provide the meaningful, responsible leadership the home requires

without being dictatorial and ignoring the wisdom and talent of his wife.'' Do you agree or disagree?

13. According to 1 Timothy 5:14 and Titus 2:4, who has been designated to guide the home?

14. Refer to the text and then discuss these necessary characteristics of a husband's role of leadership in the home:

    (1) provided in love

    (2) patterned after Christ's love for the church

    (3) provided free of bitterness

    (4) done with understanding

    (5) done in full recognition of the equality of his wife and in the sight of God

15. What are some things a husband owes his wife in his role of leadership?

16. Many women feel confused over submission. How does the message from the pulpit conflict with that gleaned from the media?

17. Conduct a poll. How many men have ever attended a class relating to the improvement of their roles as husbands?

18. How can I change my mate by changing my own attitude?

19. Why is a healthy self-image necessary for the proper roles in submission?

20. A woman does not submit *if*. She submits *because*. What is the difference?

EXERCISE

The only manner in which I can get my mate to change is by changing myself.

Husbands should list some specific ways in which they plan to treat their wives with cherishing concern as they assume their God-given roles of leadership in the home.

1. _____

2. _____

3. _____

4. _____

5. _____

Wives should note specific ways in which they plan to treat their husbands with respect and honor, thus encouraging leadership in the family.

1. _____

2. _____

3. _____

4. _____

5. _____

FEELINGS

7

Humans are complex beings. Even those who have made a profession of studying the human creature often differ dramatically with one another concerning what makes a person "tick." At some points they all throw up their hands in surrender to the unknown. Is it any wonder, then, that we often do not understand ourselves?

Not only are all humans complex, but also there are vast differences between male and female as well as a wide range of differences between individuals within these two broad categories. If I have trouble understanding myself, perhaps I feel some justification of my inability to understand others. That matter is compounded when I must cross the line and try to understand someone who, in every way, was designed by God to be different. Those who push certain causes for self-attaining ends by telling us men and women are not different are truly blind. Were they not so completely different, life would not be so marvelously mysterious (Ephesians 5:32). So while the differences make for some problems, they are interesting problems, to say the least.

Perhaps when we speak of *understanding,* we must not push the meaning to the fullest extent. Understanding that there are differences and why those differences are there constitutes the major definition. All we can add to that by way of knowledge and wisdom is simply icing on the cake. Simon Peter, by inspiration, demands men to live with their wives "according to knowledge" (1 Peter 3:7). If pushed to the ultimate meaning of *knowledge* no man would ever keep that command. When I know that my wife differs dramatically from me because she is a woman and that she is also different in many other ways because she is a unique individual, I have gone a long way in meeting God's desire in this matter. All I learn beyond this helps me to be a better husband and a better man. Beware, however, of the quest to know everything. First of all, it is unattainable; secondly, even if attained it would be at the expense of the mystique that makes the attraction between male and female so strong in the human relationship.

Man is, by nature, an analytical being. For him to understand anything, there must be logical reasons that can be spelled out in steps and brought to a *therefore* conclusion. He does not really comprehend anything else. Woman is by nature emotional and intuitive, and man's *therefore*s are not all that powerful to her. While her *feelings* are strong about many things, they do not constitute the same proof to her husband as they do to her. So to talk about *feelings* is much easier for a woman than for a man. She acts in a certain manner because of the way she feels while he feels a certain way about actions. The two draw their conclusions from opposite hemispheres of the brain, and that's the way it's supposed to be!

A wedding is a very emotional event but far more so for the bride than for the groom. In fact, most men would prefer something far less involved, without all the social hoopla. He would love her just as much and feel just as married by quietly exchanging vows in a much less emotionally charged atmosphere. Neither completely understands the view of the other concerning the wedding. After the wedding comes the marriage, and the differences of view concerning the wedding become differences that extend over a marriage of many years. A failure of either to understand means trouble multiplied with each passing year.

The society in which we live has rapidly become a society that doesn't care. "Who cares?" is today's motto. Sometimes this attitude is acquired in the family at home and exported into society. At other times it was acquired in society and imported into the home. It is, however acquired, a vicious cycle that must be broken. It will be a difficult battle. Selfishness is in man's life because of sin. That philosophy is fed by a steady diet of information from today's *experts* who tell us that we must look out for and take care of ourselves because no one else will. The reason? "No one else cares," we are told. So we have a society of sinful people built on the philosophy of *the survival of the fittest*. We are told that it is a win or lose world and that for every winner there must be a loser. It's winner take all.

The philosophy of love is an entirely different attitude. Jesus teaches us, "Do unto others as you would have them do unto you." This is the modern paraphrase of the Golden Rule. He says we do not win at the expense of another, but rather it is a shared goal gained in cooperation with another. So instead of a win/lose mentality, we have a true goal before us of win/ win. We truly win only when another wins with us. This is what real love is. That is why genuine love is so important to the success of a marriage. After all, don't the two partners become *one flesh*? How could one win at the expense of the other? "Who cares?" Everybody does where there is love.

LOVE AS A BONDING AGENT

What holds two people together when there are obviously so many differences? Love is the celestial cement that makes the two *one flesh* (Matthew 19:5). It is a *bonding agent* that comes from the combination of two ingredients—that mystique often called *sex appeal* and devotion. While both are very powerful elements, their power is multiplied to the x power when combined. The need for these two elements never ceases in marriage. The passing of years and the mellowing of age will indeed change the manner in which these elements are expressed, but the continued existence of that sexual mystique and a devotion to each that constitutes integrity and character must continue to be present and to grow in order for marriage to be the joyful, fulfilling experience God meant it to be. Contrary to popular opinion, the sexual mystique between men and women does not diminish (much less disappear) through the years. A woman always wants to be thought of and treated in terms of her femininity by a man, and a man never loses his desire to be recognized and to be treated as a man by a woman. At any age in life that's still *sex appeal.* The passing of years only deepens the devotion a man and woman have for each other. The integrity of their characters and the word of God make it so. True love is stronger in its golden years than in its green ones.

THE QUALITIES OF LOVE

SUFFERS LONG. The real meaning of the Greek word is *patience*, and it denotes patience with people rather than with situations or circumstances. There are times when we could very reasonably exact from our mates what we feel they *owe* us. We could take our own vengeance against their wrongs. So could God in His dealings with us. Inasmuch as we are all sinners (Romans 3:23; 1 John 1:8-10), God could strike us dead for any sin at any moment (as He did Ananias and Sapphira in Acts 5), but He doesn't. Why? Because He is a longsuffering God. This longsuffering is a quality of His love. We are to love with the same patience. As human beings we do try the patience of one another. Real love demands that we exercise patience. Once a lady was being interviewed about her work at the desk of the complaint department of a large store. "Don't you ever get tired of dealing with people?" she was asked. "Oh no!" she replied. "You see, I'm people too."

IS KIND. Love that is kind is sweet, useful, and helpful. It is the quality that characterized Jesus' personal ministry as "He went about doing good" (Acts 10:38). It is possible for one to be right, even righteous, and still not be kind. Mark Twain once described a man he knew as "a good man in the worst sort of way." In a hard, harsh, and brutal world Jesus was kind. Christian love is always kind.

REJOICES IN THE TRUTH. Love is able to face reality, whatever that reality might be. It rejoices in the knowledge that in dealing truthfully with every situation there is hope for a solution for every problem. Evasiveness and hypocrisy can never be substituted for truth in the name of love.

BEARS ALL THINGS. The word *bear* in the Greek could carry with it the idea of either *cover* or *endure.* Perhaps both meanings apply here. True love does cover sin. It does not pretend that sin does not exist, nor does it allow sin to be taken lightly. The cross proved once and for all that sin is not a thing to be lightly regarded. Too often we hide our heads in the sand (as the ostrich is said proverbially to do) or we make the matter of lesser consequence than it deserves. Sometimes we do this in an effort to spare someone's feelings. Often we do it to spare our own feelings. In either case there is a terrible price to be paid. Remember, though, that while these approaches will not work, there is a way in which our love can *cover* sin. In Matthew 18:15-18 Jesus taught that differences settled between two individuals alone resolves the problem without the involvement of anyone else. In James 5:16,19,20 we are taught that in loving confrontation of one who has sinned we can find healing and *cover* a multitude of sins.

When we think of this quality of love in the sense of *enduring*, it does not carry with it the idea of being burdened down with a heavy load. Enduring love is not a big pack on the back that continues to collect burdens and gets heavier and heavier. Instead the word carries with it the idea of absorbing those burdens and letting them pass through us with forgiveness. Whether it be to *cover* or *endure,* it is to be a matter of privacy and intimacy. There is no hint of gossip or of dragging into public view in the exercising of this kind of love toward our mate.

BELIEVES ALL THINGS. Love is completely trusting in each other. There is a sense in which we *make* others what we believe them to be. Constantly believing one to be lying can often lead that person to lie. The same is true of any other matter which we project onto another from our own feelings. Love always puts the best construction on every action and situation. By completely trusting our mates we help them become completely trustworthy.

HOPES ALL THINGS. The writer of the letter to the Hebrews calls hope "the anchor of the soul." Emotionally, physically, and spiritually we are doomed when we have lost all hope. Paul is reminding us here that love never loses hope. Regardless of how bad things get, there is always hope. Nothing is ever hopeless. Love keeps that hope alive and enables us to work through difficulties that otherwise would overwhelm us.

ENDURES ALL THINGS. Love's endurance is not passive but active. It does not fold its hands complacently and give in to the *inevitable*. This word calls instead for triumphant fortitude. It does not merely accept the situation but uses it redemptively. We are not meant to be the servants of problems but to make problems serve us to the glory of God!

LOVE IS A MANY SPLENDORED THING

LOVE SUFFERS LONG. The Greek word is translated *patient* and deals with patience with people as opposed to things. Because we are different our actions will be different. I am to understand that and be patient with you even when what you do is different from what I would do. When you are continually late I am to understand that *getting ready* generally takes longer for you than for me. Such preparation is often done at home where you function as *keeper* (Titus 2:5) and exercise rule. I also understand that your preparation often includes preparing children, either for this activity or for some other in place of it, and always some preparation of my things that makes my *getting ready* easier. I understand also that more last minute preparation must be made by you than by me. All these matters, when understood, help me to be more patient with you. Perhaps I could improve things by offering a little more cooperation and help.

On the other hand, perhaps you could improve the matter by understanding the same principles I understand and by trying to start preparation a little earlier so you could allot more time to it without always crossing the deadline. Husbands and wives need to be patient *with each other*; it's a two way street.

I know I try your patience with my clutter around the house, and I should be more conscientious in picking up after myself. On the other hand, the house is something we share together and our differences have to exist in love in that one house. While I appreciate your orderliness and could not live with anyone as messy as I am and am penitent about my clutter (when I notice it), I am also frustrated when orderliness goes to the point of putting a glass in the dishwasher which I just removed from the cabinet, clean, when I have merely turned to the refrigerator to get the container of juice so I can fill that glass. It's right exasperating to be hesitant to get up at night to go to the bathroom for fear I will return to find my side of the bed already *made* and ready for a new day which is several hours away. Husbands and wives need to reach a compromise they can both live with and be patient with each other in what is left.

Be patient with me in the pressures I face in a man's world and with the awesome (but joyful) responsibility of providing for the needs of my family. Give me a little respite from that pressure when I come home. I'll try to be patient with you and problems you face. I will try to sympathize if you also work outside the home. I'll try to be more helpful with the children. After all, God charged me with their care (Ephesians 6:4; Colossians 3:21). I'll be patient with your emotional days. Just give me a little time to get the world off my back first. If I am not mechanically minded, be patient with me in getting things fixed. Above all, don't attack my pride or make me feel I'm not really a man if I cannot do all such things myself. When I need nudging about anything, nudge me gently and I will strive to treat you the same way.

LOVE IS KIND. Love is not only what you do; it is what you are. Being and doing cannot be separated. Kindness is what you do for me because you love me, not because I deserve it. It is preparing my favorite meal; it is understanding my awkwardness in situations you handle quite easily; it is sensing my tiredness when you had big plans for the evening but gladly decided to spend a quiet time at home; it is accepting me for what I am and not comparing me to other men who always put me on the losing end; it is making do another year with something you really wanted to replace this year; it is your happiness with things that bring me fulfillment; it is your genuine appreciation (even if not often said openly) of what I am able to supply you by way of house, car, clothes, and the other necessities of life—something which requires most of the hours of my week and most of the years of my life. Even though I think and reason and conclude, I also have feelings. They may be less highly developed and refined than yours are, but I appreciate your kindness—your gentleness and sweetness—even when I find it hard to tell you I appreciate it.

LOVE REJOICES IN THE TRUTH. I desire your approval and encouragement when I have been open and honest with you and have honestly done my best. I want to know your love does not expect perfection but only a realistic approach and a willingness to work hard toward being a better person. This aspect of love requires meaningful communication. If there is a problem with this quality of our love, let's work together on better communication.

LOVE BEARS ALL THINGS. We are both human and love is the *muscle* that enables us to bear that. The knowledge that I am still a sinner and will be as long as I walk in the flesh makes me aware that I constantly need God's forgiveness (1 John 1:8-10) and must ask for it. I ask, though, because I know I receive it without deserving it. It comes by grace. Love must be extended to me by grace. I can never deserve your love or forgiveness. I can make it harder for you to forgive by being haughty or impenitent, but I desperately need to know you love me enough to forgive. At best it is a costly gift when you extend it. God forbid that I should raise the price either by the enormity of my sin or the attitude I hold toward it. If the problem between us is greater than you can handle alone, seek help rather than quitting or being destroyed. Make sure that turning to someone else does not take the form of gossiping about me to all your friends. Instead, talk to someone who holds your confidence as a sacred trust and will not spread the matter among others. Your love is to *cover* my sin, not make me the object of discussion all over town.

LOVE BELIEVES ALL THINGS. No one can long endure constant suspicion. I want to live my life in such a way as to deserve your confidence, and I want to know in return that you believe in me implicitly. In every area of life we must walk by faith. We must believe in the integrity, the potential, the love, and the intentions of each other. Unless you have proof to the contrary, take me at my word. Give me the benefit of the doubt.

LOVE *HOPES ALL THINGS.* When there is no hope everything is lost. We cannot go on long after hope is gone. Thankfully, few things in life are ever hopeless. Even those things pronounced *hopeless* by the experts often survive, proving the experts wrong. Few of us are qualified to call anything *"hopeless."* On the other hand, hope is the strongest medicine in the world. Prisoners of war can tell of people in apparently good health who simply lay down and died because they had lost all hope, while others seriously ill and critically injured survived and returned home because their hope remained healthy. Hope is mostly the product of our own making. Others may contribute but, in the final analysis, the result is up to us. Let's keep our relationship positive and upbeat. Let's never give up, whatever the odds. You help me and I'll help you and together hope will conquer.

LOVE ENDURES ALL THINGS. Some things in life can only be endured. These are the things that try not only our marriage but also our very souls. We must be realistic. Some things will never change. Is love strong enough to endure? Yet the *martyr complex* is not very becoming to anyone. If I must endure your endurance, the load may well be more than we both can bear. Be all you can be in spite of me. Use my weaknesses and failures as stepping stones to a bigger and better you. Good advice, isn't it? But it's far easier to give than to receive. May God grant me the same triumph. Let us never pity one another but endure one another as a means of knowing and showing God's grace. The easy way out produces no character, no strength, no glowing spiritual health. May my unchangeable weaknesses be a blessing to you and yours to me. Believe it or not, even this can make love grow stronger.

THE FEMININE VIEW
OF THE KALEIDOSCOPE

Marriage is a binding contract with or without emotions. In times past it was customary for parents to arrange the marriages of their children. Frequently neither party had even laid eyes on the other until they were brought together at the marriage ceremony. The custom still prevails in some cultures.

Most marriages today, however, are founded on emotions. Strong emotions attract male and female and then bring them to the making of vows. Those promises are intended to cement the couple while they learn to work through the problems connected with living so closely with another human being.

There is nothing wrong with emotions. The capacity to experience them is given by the Creator. We have emotions because we are emotional beings. Couples should trust one another enough to feel free to honestly say, "I'm afraid," "I'm angry," or "I love you." *Feeling* the emotion is not wrong. However, either burying a negative emotion and allowing it to smolder or fanning the fire until it rages out of control *is* wrong.

Women are usually more aware of emotions than men are. How many times has a man very logically stated his reasons for or against doing something a certain way only to have his wife respond with something such as, "I know, honey, but I just don't *feel* that it should be done like that."

DEFINITION. Much has been written concerning emotions. To read through the volumes can become tiring and a bit bewildering. Very simply stated, emotions are a person's feelings based upon his *perception* of an event or circumstances— not the facts.

Two people can experience almost identical situations and have totally different emotions. Consider, for example, the plight of a broken leg. One person who experiences such a disability may fume and fuss and make the lives of everyone around him miserable with constant complaints of "Why did this have to happen to me? It wasn't my fault. I'll be laid up for months!" Another may also break a bone but cheerfully use the convalescing time for enrichment and personal study. It is a joy to be around such a person. Both experienced very similar situations but reacted with entirely different emotions.

CONTROLLING FACTOR. While feelings are spontaneous, they are caused by one's thought patterns. We usually talk ourselves into our emotions. We produce our own misery as well as our happiness.

The writer of Proverbs had his finger on the pulse of emotions when he penned: "For as he thinketh in his heart, so is he" (Proverbs 23:7).

Negative thoughts produce negative emotions. Positive thoughts generate positive emotions. We may have very little control over what happens to us, but we do have complete control over our reaction to that event.

Facts enter our minds through our senses. We observe something by seeing, hearing, touching, smelling, or tasting. These facts are filtered through our built-in computers programmed by previous experiences, emotions, and imaginations. These filters color the experience positively or negatively. Since we reap what we sow (Galatians 6:7), we *will* get negative emotions if we sow negative thoughts. We *will* reap positive emotions from sowing positive thoughts. To try to wipe the outside of the cup and platter clean while leaving the inside covered with filth will avail nothing (Matthew 23:25,26). It is the evil from within which defiles (Mark 7:21-23).

How comforting it is to realize that God and Christ experienced the entire range of emotions and understand how we feel. "Thou understandeth my thought afar off" (Psalms 139:2). Jehovah felt grief (Genesis 6:6), hate (Deuteronomy 16:21,22), vengeance (Deuteronomy 32:35), and anger (Jeremiah 7:18,19) as well as the positive emotions of love (John 3:16) and joy (Isaiah 62:5). Christ knew anger (Mark 3:5), weeping (John 11:35; Luke 9:41), compassion (Matthew 9:36), love (John 20:2), sorrow (Matthew 26:37,38), loneliness (John 6:15), and joy (John 17:13). The Savior felt emotions but notice His complete control over them (1 Peter 2:23).

LOVE IS THE ANSWER. Love and marriage go together. While the contract is legally and morally binding without love, Paul exhorted Christian husbands to love their wives (Ephesians 5:25). Against a pagan background, these men were admonished to love their mates even as Christ loved the church—an unselfish, sacrificial love that placed the best interest of the other first.

The world's connotation of love is that of sexual attraction and romance. While both are certainly a part of love, the foundation of a marriage must involve more than lust or mere physical allurement. So many look for love from others and go around with an empty container, waiting to have it filled by someone else. Love is really a by-product of a will of the heart. In the thirteenth chapter of 1 Corinthians it is described in terms of actions. Christ showed His love for us by an action—laying down His life. In turn, we show our love for Christ by keeping His commandments (John 14;15) and by loving our brethren (John 13:35). When we are learning to love in the deepest sense of the word, we simply take the commands which God has spoken through His inspired writers and do as He instructs. We learn a new and deeper love by pushing out the old thoughts with something new. "Be ye transformed by the renewing of your mind" (Romans 12:2). "Be renewed in the spirit of your mind" (Ephesians 4:23).

"Perfect love casteth out fear" (1 John 4:18). By focusing our attention on the characteristic actions of true love, we can better understand both the positive and the negative aspects of emotions in general.

A WOMAN'S FEELINGS

April 22

LOVE SUFFERS LONG. Two people cannot live together in the bonds of marriage without trying the patience of one another very often—perhaps daily. The very closeness of the relationship is the catalyst of impatience. Love is the lubricant which smooths the rough edges.

One impediment to patience is the failure to walk in the other person's shoes. How can I possibly understand what makes you feel or act as you do unless I have faced the same circumstances through your eyes? I do not know how a man feels. I can never completely understand. But please take the time to kindly explain why you act as you do. If I better understand, no doubt my patience would increase. Another leading factor which prevents the development of patience is stress—stress in the lives of all of us. We both would do well to lessen this stumblingblock.

You try my patience when you fail to pitch in and help me when I am in a bind. I may be running behind schedule in getting the children ready to leave for some event. Seeing you sitting there in the chair, reading the paper, triggers my impatience. Don't make me beg for assistance. I am too proud. Please try to be observant and notice ways in which you can volunteer your help when I need it so desperately.

Most women express impatience over the way their husbands scatter their clothes and other possessions all over the house. True, there are extremely neat husbands and very sloppy wives. Generally speaking, however, it is the husband who is messy most of the time. Please remember that my home is an extension of myself. Try to do your fair share of picking up after yourself.

Please bear with me. I realize that I also tax your patience. You logically list the reasons for doing something a certain way only to hear my plea, "But I don't feel that is the way it should be done." I may not have a documented reason for my position. I suppose it boils down to my woman's intuition. Please take the time to study our differences and realize that emotionally I am quite complex—and a little baffling at times. You may hear me utter certain words, but try to look behind the factual meaning to the message which I am really trying to convey.

I want to be patient with you and the children. Some days there are so many demands made by the family upon my time and attention that I feel like a rubber band that has been stretched as far as it will go without breaking. And then there are days when I feel as if the band has snapped.

LOVE IS KIND. Kindness is a universal language. Everyone understands its meaning. Kindness says, "I know I don't have to do this and it really isn't expected, but I want to because I think so much of you!" Slowly, day by day, we lay the bricks of kind deeds which eventually build a strong and healthy marriage.

Sometimes kindness is based as much on what you don't do as what you do. Perhaps I have ruined a meal. You could simply state the facts and crush me. How I love you for smoothing over my mistakes and ignoring the obvious when you come to the table. Maybe I have gained a few pounds recently. It would be so easy for you to tease me. Instead, you never mentioned it.

Gifts at traditional times are more or less expected. Perhaps we all take them for granted. However, I love to receive little surprises throughout the year. They need not be expensive. In fact, I had rather that they not be. The awareness that you heard me mention something I would like to have and then got it for me means more than I can tell. Maybe I did not say a word, but you sensed that the surprise would mean a lot.

In its deepest sense, kindness has nothing to do with material things. You may provide a lovely home, a car, adequate medical care, and sufficient insurance. I realize that this is your way of expressing love but such manifestations can be hard, cold facts without the magic of kindness. I want you to be sweet to me. I want you to be kind. Kindness can be a glance; a wink; holding the door open for me; pulling out my chair; saying something complimentary about me in the presence of others; taking me out when you sense that I am down in spirits; or offering to keep the children so I can have some time out of the house.

Kindness is all the little things you do that say, "You're special. I love you, honey!"

LOVE REJOICES IN THE TRUTH. Sometimes the truth can be quite painful. The glare hurts our eyes so we cover them. It is easier to hide behind a facade of pleasantries than it is to honestly tell one another how we feel. But real love does not play "Let's pretend." We cannot love a sham. If love is to endure, it must be willing to strip off the veneer and stand there completely bare.

I can better tell you how I honestly feel if you seem open and receptive. If I sense that you disapprove, then I will undoubtedly devise all sorts of protective devices to spare myself the hurt. I may pout. I may give you the silent treatment. I may blissfully act as if nothing is wrong for years. If I evade the truth, then you love my act instead of me.

Remember one very fundamental principle. We must learn the art of telling the truth in kindness. I do not want to feel humiliated for being honest about my feelings. Neither do I as the listener want to feel inferior when the truth exposes my own weaknesses. We should strive to welcome hearing the truth and also to learn how to express it in kindness.

LOVE BEARS ALL THINGS. Two people who live together in the closeness of the marriage relationship will inevitably have differences of opinions and some conflict. Sometimes we should talk with a concerned third party in order to resolve our problems. Most of the time, however, we can more effectively work through our controversies if we have not flaunted them before family, friends, and community.

Please do not make fun of my weaknesses. I have many. Do not hold them up to ridicule before our friends. To tell others that I am a poor cook will not make me a better one.

When you laughingly remark, even to casual acquaintances concerning my poor spending habits, I feel only resentment— not a desire to learn better management. Frequently women are the violators of this fundamental principle of love. We generally express our feelings more easily than men do. We may more often be guilty of parading our disagreements before others instead of bearing with them, or covering them, until we have had opportunity to triumphantly work our way through any hindrances.

We do not deny conflict. Instead, you, God, and I quietly bear some problems until we have had ample time to find solutions.

LOVE BELIEVES ALL THINGS. Please believe in me. I will make many mistakes. There are times when I let you down. I am only human.

So are you.

Don't lose faith in me. Believe that I am a person of worth. Tell me so. My feelings of self-worth are learned primarily as I see them reflected in the eyes of others. And it is your eyes that I see when I first awaken each morning. Your eyes are also the last ones I view before the lights are turned out at night. If you feel that I am beautiful, then I will see that reflection and believe it. If you think that I am a kind and loving wife, then I will strive with every fiber of my being to live up to your expectations. When you run me down and criticize me before others, I usually also live up to those expectations in the long run.

How well I remember a time when your belief in my returning to a normal life—when all the odds were against me— was the underlying strength for recovery. When legs wouldn't work, you patiently supported me as I stumbled around the house, learning to use those muscles again. Your words, "Now it's your turn to walk on your own," expressed your belief that I would walk. And I did.

LOVE HOPES ALL THINGS. The marriage vows are the mortar that holds the walls together until they become firm. There has to be a commitment that both parties will hang in there through thick and thin. Husband and wife have to hope that eventually all things will work out.

Without that hope, divorce could easily seem inevitable to those with no convictions. Almost any married couple of long standing could relate several instances when they were so upset with one another that they could have easily called it quits. This is especially true when one partner has injured the inner core of the other. It is only basic human instinct to fight for survival.

Hope says, "We have made a commitment. Problems will have to be worked out, but we *will* find a way." When one or both parties begin envisioning that there is no hope, then it becomes increasingly difficult to ever work on the disagreements.

It seems that a woman, even more than a man, longs for the security that the marriage will last. There is something about her basic temperament that yearns for the assurance that a problem does not mean the end of a relationship. It's just a rock for climbing!

LOVE ENDURES ALL THINGS. Some situations we bear. We quietly keep them between ourselves and God with the full expectations or hope that we will work our way through whatever problems may exist.

We endure some difficulties, however, in the truest sense of the word. Some circumstances in marriage may cause real emotional pain. There is a deep hurting. There is anguish. But two people who love one another are committed to each other and their marriage. They do not endure in resignation just because there is no other alternative. They endure problems because they realize that, with God's help, they can be victorious.

CONCLUSION

It must be obvious by now that if marriage is to succeed and bring its joy and happiness into our lives, there must be love. And that love must be expressed in a caring and concerned way. Of what value is unexpressed love? Here are several ways a caring, concerned husband or wife expresses love. Check your own actions and see if you are truly loving your mate.

1. *VERBAL EXPRESSION*. Those who find it easy to converse usually have no difficulty saying, "I love you." They may hardly ever say it, but it's not because they can't. Others have much more difficulty in conversing about any topic. To them these words come hard. But verbal expression of love is a strong vitamin when injected into the life of another.

2. *MATERIAL EXPRESSION*. Our treasure is put where our heart is. When money is available and little or none of it is invested in love for the other, there is a strong suspicion that love is absent. The items don't have to be expensive but money spent on gifts of love speaks loudly of our devotion.

3. *NON-MATERIAL SUPPORT*. We have so much to give that does not fall into the category of words or money: things such as encouragement, backing, and listening. Does your love for husband or wife involve you in these areas? We must be sensitive to such needs and respond with care and concern. Patience is also a quality that belongs in this category. All the things we have mentioned under this heading involve the second of man's most valuable treasures—his time. In short, are we willing to invest the time in our marriage that will nurture it and help it grow? Sometimes it is a matter of maintenance. Nearly everything in life must be maintained and that means both time and money. Cars need it, houses need it, lawns need it, appliances need it; marriage needs maintenance also. Be concerned enough to invest.

4. *SELF-EXPOSURE*. How sad it is when husband and wife are not truly best friends. It is regrettable that

others often know more about the real person inside the body of our mate than we do. Have you shown your mate your soul? Does he or she know how you really feel about the deep and basic issues in your life? If not, is it because you are afraid of such disclosure or perhaps the suspicion or realization that the other doesn't really care? One who is not loved as he truly *is* simply is not loved at all. All too often we love the character that is being portrayed instead of the real person who is playing that part. Love a real person. Be a real person.

5. *INTIMACY*. Intimacy means far more than sexual intercourse. It is holding hands on a walk. It is a gentle touch of the cheek or caress of the hand. It is a look in the eye that can be detected all the way across a crowded room. These must all be non-demanding in nature. They may indeed be a prelude to sexual intercourse, one of the deepest and truest of all expressions of love, but not always so. Not even usually so. They then become demanding and self-serving, even threatening. When a wife uses intimacy only to get her way about a matter or a husband uses it only as a means of getting his wife in bed with him, they have destroyed its spontaneous nature.

6. *RESPECT FOR INDIVIDUALITY*. The fact that in marriage two become one flesh does not mean either person loses his identity by being absorbed into the other. There are still two individuals and each one is a whole person. There is real strength in the individuals, and thus in the marriage, when both are able to retain their individuality and function well apart from each other. There is deep love for one another and genuine joy in shared experiences, but neither is threatened by being alone or functioning independently. True love not only respects that individuality but actively cultivates it. The demands of an altogether togetherness are selfish and put an undue strain on marriage. Separate

hobbies, separate work, separate identities bring a healthy wholesomeness to the marriage and enable each one to contribute the best of themselves to that relationship. If I cannot respect the separate personality and separate interest of my partner in marriage, something is wrong with my love. If I like to hike or hunt but she enjoys reading or writing, neither should attempt to make the other feel guilty when pursuing personal interests. After all, there will be many common interests and the spaces in our togetherness make the common interests that much more precious and enjoyable.

7. *EMOTIONAL BONDING*. Togetherness does not necessarily produce emotional bonding. Some couples share a golden wedding anniversary without ever having come to really know each other or forming the deep emotional bonds that truly make us one. While togetherness can smother when wrongly used or demanded, that same togetherness, in the proper amounts and proper ways, can produce a tie between individuals that nothing can break. Shared hobbies or time spent together in the same room with the wall or television between does not produce the deep cohesive bonds that marriage is supposed to cultivate. Some of this bonding takes place in the deep emotions of sexual intimacy and its associated warmth and affection. Worship and other religious activities shared together help build these bonds. The rearing of children together, with both participating in teaching and discipline, is a deeply satisfying part of marriage that binds couples closer. Cooperative management of the finances of the marriage gives both a sense of worth and accomplishment that draws them closer together. Social activities that involve best friends of both or families of both are actions that bond.

Make your love the right quality and you'll know and appreciate the family meaning of the phrase, ''Blest be the tie that binds.'' Such a tie is not a chain but a wonderful cohesion—a mystical bond that makes two people one flesh yet allows (even seeks and cultivates) individuality. Ask yourself, then answer honestly, ''Do I really love my life's partner?''

SUGGESTIONS FOR CLASS DISCUSSION
Chapter 7

1. Suggest some ways in which people differ from one another as individuals. How do men and women generally differ?

2. First Peter 3:7 admonishes men to live with their wives ''according to knowledge.'' What does that phrase mean?

3. What are the two ingredients in love, the bonding agent of marriage? *sex appeal & devotion*

4. In discussing the qualities of love, what is a synonym for ''suffers long''? *patience*

5. Love is to be ''kind.'' How can one be righteous and yet not be kind?

6. Love ''rejoices in the truth.'' What part does the truth play in marriage? *page 84*

7. Love ''bears all things.'' The original word for *bears* means to *cover* or *endure*. Discuss the thoughts presented on this concept in the lesson.

8. The idea behind the words ''believes all things'' is trust. How can trusting our mates help them become trustworthy?

9. Love ''hopes all things.'' Is any marriage ever truly hopeless?

10. Love ''endures all things.'' What is the meaning of ''endure''?

11. Under the headings of "Love Is a Many Splendored Thing" and "A Woman's Feelings," seven characteristics of love are discussed from the viewpoints of both a man and a woman. Compare their differences and similarities.

12. What is your opinion of the definition of the word *emotions* in the statement: "Emotions are a person's feelings based upon his perception of an event or circumstances— not the facts"?

13. Give examples of two people facing the same set of circumstances and yet experiencing different emotions. How does this affect a marriage?

14. Since our emotions are primarily caused by our thought patterns, what is the logical solution for controlling our emotions?

EXERCISE

Seven suggestions were made for expressing love to your partner. Each day this week try to find an occasion to use each of the suggestions. Count one point for each expression of love every time you use it. Total your points at the end of the week.

		Total
1. Verbal Expression	_____	_____
2. Material Expression	_____	_____
3. Non-material Support	_____	_____
4. Self-exposure	_____	_____
5. Intimacy	_____	_____
6. Respect for Individuality	_____	_____
7. Emotional Bonding	_____	_____
	Grand Total	_____

May 6.

WHEN THE HOUSE IS BUILT
ON SAND

8

Regardless of where or how we build our lives, they must all withstand some very rigorous testing. Jesus taught us to build upon the foundation of solid rock. Even there rains, winds, and floods will assail us but we have the confident assurance of being able to weather the storms. Nothing is said of it being either easy or pleasant to face such trials. We are, however, assured of survival when we have built properly. Pity the poor man, though, who faces such adversity without a proper foundation. The failure factor is built in (Matthew 7:26).

The true foundation for all building is respect for and obedience to the authority of God. That authority, however, extends into many areas. For that reason foundations may be part stone and part sand. Let's examine some situations where sand has been substituted for rock and see the necessity of digging out the sand and replacing it with that which is substantial. A failure to do so threatens the very existence of our house.

Some think that money is a solid foundation. How many young women have sought a *professional* man for a husband in the belief that his substantial income will insure happiness for both of them? How many young men have married a girl because she is the heir to a family fortune? Paul warns against the love of money (1 Timothy 6:10) and the will to be rich (1 Timothy 6:9). There are many things money cannot buy and it can buy none of the things that bring true happiness: love, respect, faithfulness, companionship. Paul is right when he concludes that pursuit of money pierces one through with many sorrows and eventually causes the loss of the soul (1 Timothy 6:10).

Even with living proof everywhere in abundance that money does not buy happiness, many still build on the foundation of materialism. How often when there is strife, discontent, and unhappiness do people conclude that some material possession would cure everything? So they buy a new car, or a boat, or a house, or new clothes—the list is endless. The original problem remains unsolved and new ones have been added: How am I to pay for what I've purchased? Often newlyweds want to start at the top with as much or more than their parents possess after twenty-five or thirty years of gradual accumulations. Almost as often, parents help create that problem by rushing to the rescue of their children in every little problem. This not only deprives the young of developing the willpower and muscle of survival but it also fans the flames of material appetite. Mothers and fathers see some difficulty in the life of a child and assume that helping them buy that house, or car, or boat will solve the problem. It rarely does because the problem goes deeper than some material possession. In Psalms 127:1,2 David tells us that every house not built by the Lord is built in vain and it is therefore vain to get up early and stay up late in order to try to salvage it by taking on two jobs. Many couples hardly know each other because they work so hard to try to make enough money to pay for all they have bought to make them happy that they have no time left for each other or for the things they have purchased.

In a recent article on aviation accidents, one thing caught my eye. The number one cause of crashes of small aircraft is overloading. Loaded beyond their capacity, they fail. Many marriages fail for the same reason. It is ironic that the very things people think will make them happy and solve their problems actually become bigger problems and the source of much unhappiness. Look around you and see the debris of the crashes caused by overloading. We can avoid tragedy by learning through the experiences of others. Sadly, many seem to be able to learn only through their own experiences and sometimes not even then. Once two hunters chartered an airplane and pilot to take them into the wilderness of northern

Canada on an elk hunt. It was agreed by the hunters and the pilot that he would return in ten days to pick them up. Ten days later he landed and two men were waiting with two elk they had killed. The pilot informed them that they could fly out with only one elk because the load capacity of the plane would be exceeded by three men and two elk. The hunters objected. One said, "The pilot who picked us up last year had a plane just like yours and he let us take two elk." The pilot thought the matter over and concluded that maybe he was too safety conscious. Maybe he had underestimated the ability of his plane. Finally the two elk and three men were aboard but the plane labored to get airborne. Try as he would, the plane could gain no altitude and finally made a crash landing. Realizing their plight, sitting there disabled in the middle of nowhere, the irate pilot asked, "Do you know where we are?" One of the hunters replied, "Well, not exactly, but as best as I can figure we are about five miles from where we crashed last year." Lessons not learned by experience are destined to be repeated.

A woman discovered that the apartment she and her husband had leased was shared by another tenant—a mouse. The husband bought a trap that would catch the mouse humanely. Having caught the mouse they were now faced with the problem of disposing of it. Not wishing to kill it with a hammer or in some other violent way, they decided they would drown it. They filled a bucket with water, dropped the trap into the bucket and stepped outside for a few minutes until the ordeal was over. To their surprise they discovered when they returned that the water was not deep enough and that, by standing on tiptoe, the mouse was able to barely keep its nose above the water. The woman concluded, "All at once I saw a picture of myself. In an effort to find happiness I had surrounded myself with things I had purchased. Like the water surrounding the cage, I had been trapped by them. I was exhausted from constantly standing on tiptoe in an effort to breathe. These possessions were not making me happy; they were suffocating me. Now I was destined to work myself to death to try to pay for them."

Why is money such a problem when the Lord Himself said, " . . . a man's life consisteth not in the abundance of the things which he possesseth"? The first reason is obvious: many people simply do not believe what the Lord said! Of course there are many reasons people fail to believe the Lord's teaching.

1. We live in a materially oriented world where pressures to buy and own are tremendous. Even the philosophy of government is that a strong national economy can exist only in a strong consumer market. So pressure is exerted on every hand to buy, buy, buy. We even build obsolescence into products so the same products can be sold over and over again to the same customers. Commercials are of such nature as to create a tremendous thirst for things. Yet the things are like salt water. They do not quench the thirst; they create stronger thirst.

2. We measure self-worth by money. Why do many resort to such a drastic measure as taking their own lives when they face a great financial loss? To them the loss is not financial. It is a loss of face, of self, of respect. They feel such financial loss is a destruction of what they are. In truth such loss only takes what you have. It has no way of touching what you are. It is, though, a great revealer of what you are. Perhaps it is that revelation that drives some to desperation.

3. Money and material things are a symbol of power. Many lust for power more than anything else in this world. Those with money feel they have great power and those without it feel powerless. But the greatest powers in the world are untouched either by the presence or absence of money.

With such ideas firmly implanted in the mind, is it any wonder that two human beings come into conflict over money? We are all sinful (Romans 3:23), and the root of sin is selfishness. Most couples find it difficult to talk about money unselfishly. Both partners usually feel their view of the situation is the right view and are resentful when there isn't enough money to go around or they don't get their own way in the allocation and spending of it. That resentment is often expressed in such statements as, "You don't trust me," or "You don't love me," or "You don't understand me."

Today's world is quite different to that of a generation or two ago. Today nearly sixty percent of wives are employed and account for at least thirty percent of the income of the household. By the turn of the century, eighty percent of wives will be employed and will earn nearly fifty percent of the family income. In this new society, traditional and cultural ways of past generations must give way to new traditions and customs.

Surprisingly, for many people the problem is not a lack of money but too much of it! A couple with a joint income of only $30,000 a year will earn more than a million dollars during the years of their marriage. In that sense, most married couples are millionaires but with little wisdom and expertise in handling such funds. Fortunately, you don't have to handle it all at one time but in much smaller increments.

There are some important guidelines to follow in the management of money in order to keep it from becoming a major problem and a sandy foundation in the marriage.

First, both must realize that, in spite of all the money earned in a lifetime, there is never enough at any one time to cover all the *wants*. By the very nature of our society, most will find their wants bigger than the amount of money can supply. Therefore, there must be mutual agreement that both will have to do without some things. Any other course spells disaster.

Second, both must participate in supplying and allocating the funds necessary to the running of the household. This must be done prior to spending the money. It does little good to *cry over spilled milk* or argue over where the money has gone after it has already been spent. This means budgeting. Amazingly, many couples, though they argue over spent money, do not really know where or how it was spent. They have no planned budget and keep no accurate records. No wonder so many complain of money problems in marriage.

Third, each must assume responsibility for the running of certain portions of the household. Both share in major decisions and pay their agreed share out of an account in their name. There's good reason for this. It gives both a tangible symbol of their responsibility. Money paid out of their account usually receives more consideration than that paid out of a joint account. In this way there is no cheating and drawing against your spouse's account when you have mismanaged your own. Each person also needs the psychological benefit of exercising some control over the money earned.

Fourth, each needs some money that belongs to him or to her to do with as they please. It must not be excessive, but each needs to feel the independence of being able to do some things without asking or begging the permission of the other. These cannot, of course, be major things. But in other matters each needs to feel trust from their mate and personal self-confidence to handle small affairs.

This may sound strange to the customs and traditions characteristic of the generation in which you grew up, but is it unscriptural? Before you answer, perhaps you need to read the story of the worthy woman in Proverbs 31. Maybe you need to ask if Lydia's conversion in Acts 16 included going out of business.

Money is a necessary part of our lives, but we must learn to use it as a servant and not a master. We dare not allow a wrong attitude toward money to become the material out of which we build our marriages.

Physical attraction and sexual desire make a poor foundation if they alone constitute the foundation. While both are important and are blessings of God intended to bring joy, they are not capable of being the entire foundation. Neither man nor woman can live on sex alone. Make sure that the ingredient is there, but make certain also that it is accompanied by many other important building stones.

People marry for a number of different reasons: a desire to escape, loneliness, a desire to have children, pressure from others, a desire to exercise dominion over the life of someone else, and a host of other reasons. None of these alone can support a home. Build on the rock. What you are building affects both time and eternity.

Much of what many people believe about marriage is simply not true. It is a hoax, a fraud, *an old wives' tale,* or a *chimney corner scripture.* Yet many persist in saying, "We hold these truths to be self-evident." How much suffering and heartache exist because of these, and still they have more lives than the proverbial cat. It seems impossible to kill them. Instead, we let them kill us or our marriage. How many of these myths do you believe or have you believed in the past? How many have you passed on to others? If ever rotten materials existed for a foundation, these are among them:

1. All people get married because they love each other.

2. All married people have a romantic love.

3. A happy marriage means there is lot of romantic love.

4. A perfect sexual relationship will develop easily and automatically.

5. A perfect sexual relationship is perfect technique.

6. If the sexual relationship is great, other problems will solve themselves.

7. If there are problems in the sexual relationship, you have problems elsewhere.

8. Loneliness will be cured by getting married.

9. Your partner in marriage will satisfy all your emotional and social needs.

10. The more time husbands and wives spend together, the better the marriage.

11. Marriage is an excellent way to change or reform a person.

12. If a marriage has a rough time to start with, it will automatically improve with time.

13. A marriage with problems will automatically improve by having a baby.

14. Any disagreement between husband and wife is always detrimental.

15. Couples who love each other know intuitively all the other's needs and wants.

Many major social studies over a period of years have proven that happily married people function more successfully in every other realm of life. They live longer, they resist disease better, they live more stable emotional lives. Does that surprise us? It shouldn't. The home is the foundation and basic building block of society. Solve the ills of the home and you solve most other problems. Children reared in unstable homes perpetuate instability in society. They are lacking in stability and establish homes that, in turn, produce more unstable people and consequently more problems. *WE SIMPLY MUST DEAL WITH THE PROBLEMS AND ILLS OF THE HOME, OR WE ARE DESTINED TO BRING UTTER DESTRUCTION TO OUR SOCIETY!*

In this discussion nothing has been said about unscriptural marriages. The reason is obvious. Such "marriages" are not marriages at all. There is no way to repair the foundation because both the foundation and building itself are condemned. There is no hope for it. It must be destroyed. In this category would be active homosexuals, previously married people with no scriptural divorce, and other such deviates from God's norm. Be sure to consult the blueprint carefully before even thinking about starting to build. It is much better and wiser to never build at all than to build improperly.

Another problem arises when a couple tries to build a new home within an existing one. While there is a place, an important place, for kin on both sides, care must be taken to avoid making them problems instead of blessings.

Much of what we accept in both the wedding and the marriage which follows comes from past tradition. Some of these traditions we have never even heard discussed, and others we know and yet fail to note their connection with present day life.

"Who gives this woman away?" the preacher may ask as the wedding ceremony starts. Usually it is the father of the bride who answers, "Her mother and I." (In one wedding in which I officiated the excited father replied, "*My* mother and I.") Are you aware of the custom behind this? In many cultures the bride is, in reality, given by her family to the groom and his family. She literally moves from one family to another. Often it involves the paying of a *bride price* dowry as she and her husband live with his family, often a large clan.

Yet in the same ceremony is the phrase, "For this cause shall a man leave his father and mother and be joined to his wife," words connecting us to Hebrew tradition as recorded both in the Old and New Testaments of the Bible. Confusing, isn't it! But it's not the words that lead to the confusion and trouble experienced in the modern marriage when it comes to kin. In fact, most people do not even remember what they said in their marriage vows. The problems come from the situations that arise out of day-to-day living. Should two families live in the same house? Should the newly established family expect or accept financial aid from either of the families from which they came? How much advice or criticism should they accept from either family? How much time should be spent with the other family? How should time be shared for holidays? Should grandparents be expected or allowed to "help rear" the children? These are very real issues that must be satisfactorily resolved by both husband and wife. These are *their* problems, and *they* must solve them in a way that will satisfy themselves. Family interests on both sides must be secondary. Blessed is the family that can settle these issues to the general satisfaction of everyone involved. That's easier said than done. Problems with the extended family can be allowed to wreck a marriage. Make sure this part of your marriage is built on solid ground.

It is possible, however, to make this problem bigger than life. Much has been said about this aspect of marriage that is false (like the typical mother-in-law jokes), and many myths have been accepted as truth. It is not true that every married person has trouble with in-laws. In fact, social studies reveal that more than half of the married people interviewed experienced no trouble with their in-laws, and many reported better relationships with in-laws than with their own families.

What has been said concerning the extended family can also be said of close friendships of both bride and groom. Both had friends before marriage, so what happens now to those relationships? Both still need friendships in order to be well-rounded socially and emotionally. If someone in this category is a particular problem to your mate, some satisfactory adjustment must be made.

Remember two things: you need family and friends and they need you; but your marriage takes precedence over anybody or anything else.

Both husband and wife must be sensible, cooperative, considerate, and willing to make some compromises in these areas. Discuss these matters openly and frankly with one another so there is no misunderstanding. Then let each be determined to do what's best to build a good marriage.

LET'S SUMMARIZE

1. The key to all happy relationships is mutual submission (Ephesians 5:21).

2. There must be full recognition of equality and respect for one another.

3. Many troubled marriages could be cured by an attitude adjustment.

4. Mutual submission is not belittling to any of the parties involved.

5. God-given roles never change but customs and traditions do; therefore, we must never confuse the two.

6. Marriage can and should be a happy and rewarding relationship. Never be satisfied by playing "let's pretend."

SUGGESTIONS FOR CLASS DISCUSSION
Chapter 8

1. Regardless of the foundation, every marriage is tested by winds, rains, and floods. Discuss some examples. What is the built-in failure factor of Matthew 7:26?

2. The true foundation for all building is respect for and obedience to the authority of God. Why are some foundations part stone and part sand?

3. What is the primary peril of a marriage built on a foundation of money?

4. What is the difference between the love of money in 1 Timothy 6:10 and the will to be rich mentioned in verse 9 of the same chapter?

5. What are some things that money cannot buy?

6. How does the love of money eventually cause the loss of the soul (1 Timothy 6:10)?

7. Do you agree or disagree with the thought that many newlyweds expect to begin marriage with the same standard of living which required their parents twenty-five or thirty years to attain? Are the parents partially responsible for this attitude?

8. Relate the examples of the elk hunters and the mouse to the problem of materialism.

9. What is the primary reason that money is such a problem in marriages when the Lord said, "... a man's life consisteth not in the abundance of the things which he possesseth"?

10. What are some of the pressures put upon people to buy and spend more and more? How are material possessions like salt water?

11. In what ways is self-worth measured by money?

12. How are material things a symbol of power?

13. Compare the number of employed women in this generation with the previous one. Is this good or bad? What are the complications?

14. Do you agree or disagree with the statement that the problem is often too much money instead of a lack of it?

15. Discuss the four guidelines in the management of money.

16. Some marriages are built primarily upon physical attraction and sexual desire. Is there anything wrong with either of these being in the foundation? What should be their place?

17. Discuss the fifteen misconceptions concerning marriage that were presented in the lesson.

18. Can anything be done about unscriptural "marriages"? Give scriptures for your answer.

19. What is the cultural basis for the words, "Who gives this woman away?" often found at the beginning of a wedding ceremony?

20. What are some of the problems in a marriage involving relatives? What problems stem from close friendships of both bride and groom? What is the answer?

IDENTITY CONFLICTS — WHICH AM I?

9

One of the great myths in marriage is that happily married couples have no conflicts.

"We have been married for forty-five years and have never had a disagreement!"

We have all heard statements such as the one above. There may be a marriage such as this—somewhere. Some husbands and wives have short memories. Others deliberately lie in an effort to cover up their conflicts. One partner may be so domineering that the other dares not voice an opinion. Some have gone their separate ways for so long that neither one sees the other long enough to disagree. The more fortunate ones learned the art of resolving differences so many years ago that they are no longer even aware that they are using this skill.

Conflicts are normal. It would be difficult indeed for two people as different as male and female to live under the same roof and not clash in their opinions from time to time. A happy marriage is not one free from conflict. Neither is it one in which both partners are alike. Instead, it is one in which both husband and wife have gradually learned to resolve these differences with a minimum of hurt to either one. Conflict resolution thus becomes an automatic response.

So often we tend to major in minors. A mate has an irritating trait which becomes blown out of proportion through the years. Sometimes it helps just to sit down together and identify what our differences are. They may be in the realm of politics, hobbies, food preferences, clothes, recreation, time spent with friends or relatives, cars, place to spend a vacation, internal timetables for getting things done, etc.

Putting such differences down on paper and openly discussing them can be most enlightening. Be sensible. How

many of these differences are critical in your marriage? Some
we simply learn to live with. Others are of such disruptive
force that they must be successfully dealt with if the marriage
is to be a good one.

These general suggestions may be helpful in learning to
deal with differences.

1. **TOLERATE**. It is impossible for two completely different people to live in the same house in the closeness
   of the marriage relationship without some sort of friction. For example, one could be an outdoor sports
   enthusiast while the other loves to curl up with a good
   book by the fire. This should present no major problem for two mature people. They can simply learn to
   agree to disagree. Nothing is wrong with either prefer-
   ence. Each should feel free to pursue his or her own
   interests with the full blessing of the other.

   One loves corned beef and cabbage. The other
   detests the dish. There is absolutely nothing wrong
   with having two different main dishes once every six
   months or so.

   Remember that your success in marriage is not
   measured by your similarities, but rather by how well
   you learn to tolerate your differences.

2. **ROTATE**. In every marriage there has to be some give
   and take. Neither partner should get his or her way all
   the time. It is equally as devastating when one or both
   refuse to ever give in out of sheer stubbornness. Especially in the realm of minor issues, it is only fair to take
   turns in getting one's way. For example, there may
   well be a conflict concerning which television program
   to watch. Rather than have a constant argument, how
   much more sensible it is to agree to alternate weeks in
   viewing a favorite program.

3. **NEGOTIATE**. Sometimes it is best to live side by
   side, tolerating one another's differences. In other situations the solution seems to lie in taking turns so that

each one may have what he or she wishes part of the time. On the other hand, there are times when neither of these methods of solving conflicts will help. Both husband and wife must give up the idea of having his or her own way, even on an alternating basis, and must reach an agreement on a compromise that will be suitable to each. For example, one partner would love to save fifty percent of each paycheck. The other gleefully spends every dime. Obviously there can be no harmony when each has his or her own way. It would be difficult to take turns in spending. Logically they must sit down and negotiate. Each one agrees to go to a spending level that was not the original choice of either, but one that they both can live with. The conservative one may have to learn to be content with saving only ten percent of the income, remembering that even this amount seems staggering to the spender.

MARITAL IRRITATIONS

Since we *are* different, our spouses will frequently do or say things which irritate us. Sometimes we can honestly shrug it off. There are other times when these little grains of sand are truly annoying. Rather than allow them to build up to volcanic proportions, it is far better to deal with them in a kind manner on a day-to-day basis.

Each couple's list will vary, but these are some common points of friction:

1. You always leave your towel on the bathroom floor.

2. You made us late again.

3. You made fun of me in front of friends.

4. You contradicted what I told the children to do.

5. You promised me that you would fix the dripping faucet a month ago.

6. You joked about the problem when I tried to talk to you.

7. You were not supposed to tell anyone. I talked to you in confidence.

8. You keep bringing up silly mistakes that I made ten years ago.

9. You spent too much money.

10. You always wait until the last minute.

Frequently one partner may not even be aware that his or her behavior is adversely affecting the other one. When proper lines of communication have been opened, it should be a simple matter to gently let a mate know that a certain practice or habit annoys you. But remember that the other party has the same right!

CASE STUDIES

TEARS. Yesterday Mary was joking and seemed to be in great spirits. Tom teased her somewhat about the overcooked dinner which she served. They had a good laugh over the matter and there seemed to be no problems.

Today was a different story. His first cheerful words upon entering the house were, "Honey, are we having burnt sacrifices tonight like we did yesterday?" The remainder of the evening was flooded with tears. Tom could not understand. He had made only one innocent remark. Mary herself had laughed over the same situation the evening before.

Tom failed to realize that whereas the chemical balance in his own body remains fairly stable, that of Mary's body fluctuates drastically. She may have a surge of hormones released into her blood stream overnight. The very same event which prompted laughter the day before could easily produce weeping upon the dawning of a new day. Simply telling her that there is no reason to cry will not stop the tears. Hormones filling her entire system tell her to weep. She has very little control.

Simply understanding the biological principles involved is half the battle. While Tom could be a bit more sensitive in the teasing of Mary, he should be aware of the fact that she, in all likelihood, would have cried over *anything* he had said on that particular day. When a couple dwells together according to knowledge, each must be aware of the overwhelming emotional effects and refuse to take the consequences as a personal insult. The knowledge that *this, too, shall pass* should be valuable while waiting for conditions to change.

* * * * * *

JOB VERSUS HOUSE. Jerry was elated. The promotion that he had waited for had finally been offered. Imagine! A move across the country and his very own office as vice president of the company. His feet were barely touching the stairs as he raced in the door to share the excitement with Karen. A promotion. A new house. A new community. New friends. A new school for the children. It was great!

Jerry lifted Karen off the floor in his arms as the news of his promotion and the upcoming move tumbled from his heart and mouth in words which were too inadequate to convey his joy.

Her facial expression was frozen. There were no gleeful words—only a look of dismay and disbelief.

"Honey, aren't you happy? The years of college night classes. All the unpaid hours of overtime. All the paper work I have brought home so I could be eligible for a promotion. At last it has paid off! I'm a *somebody*. I'm a success in my career. This is what we have talked about so much. It is what we have planned for and dreamed about ever since we have been married. Why aren't you saying anything? Why do you look so sad?"

Karen may not say much of anything for days. She is not really sure of her own feelings. Her intellect informs her that she should be grateful. But some hidden emotion has jammed her thought waves. Finally the trouble surfaces. Karen does not want to leave her house. Its comforting walls have supportingly wrapped themselves around her to such an extent that she dreads leaving the security. How will her children feel in a new school? Who will run errands for her aging parents? How she dreads to pull up her comfortable roots and begin life anew.

The two conflicts met in a head-on collision. Jerry's job was an extension of himself. Many of his lifetime goals centered around advancing in his career. Karen's extension of herself lay in her home and family. Pulling up roots from everything near and dear to her seemed devastating.

Jerry and Karen will never be able to handle this situation until they can first express their true feelings about the matter. His natural ambitions and her just-as-natural yearnings for security through her home must be reckoned with and handled in a compromising manner.

*   *   *   *   *   *

ADULT TOYS. Martha was furious. Kevin had just bought another new rifle. He purchased one last year also. And the year before that. Last summer it was a new boat. This summer it was new fishing equipment. Martha had had nothing new for herself for two years.

Kevin could not understand Martha's selfishness. After all, she had new carpets installed throughout the house last year. The old draperies did not match so new ones were necessary. She wanted the cute pink wallpaper and got it. The old washing machine fell apart and had to be replaced by a new one. If she could have new carpets, draperies, wallpaper, and a washing machine, then why couldn't he have some equipment for his hunting and fishing?

Martha failed to realize that the little boy in Kevin wanted some *toys* to continue his play in the adult world. At the same time, she could not see that she was continuing her childhood diversion of playing house through her home. Both Martha and Kevin need to mature to the extent that they can see behind the facades which mask their actual feelings. After an understanding of one another's true emotions is reached, both need to be mature enough to compromise.

* * * * * *

LOGIC OR EMOTION. Pam was excited. She had discovered the most beautiful outfit while she was shopping. And it was on sale. A real bargain! She could hardly wait to show it to Tom.

As soon as he arrived home from work, Pam ran to the bedroom and slipped into her new clothes. Proudly modeling them, she asked her husband what he thought.

Tom thought the color was wrong and the fit was a poor one. Anyway, they really could not afford the purchase right now—bargain or not. And he told her so. Pam ran out of the room sobbing. Tom was bewildered. After all, she had asked him a simple question, ''How do you like it?'' Since she had asked, he logically told her the truth as he saw it, pointing out three good reasons. Why was she upset? If she had not wanted his opinion, then she should not have asked. He had only made a logical response.

Tom and Pam both failed to understand that men and women simply do not reason alike. A man may list his reasons for or against something in a purely logical manner. Pam was not looking for a court case of logical reasoning. She had found an outfit that made her feel good about herself. When she asked Tom what he thought about it, she was not looking for logic. She simply wanted his approval for a decision which she had already made. A woman's initial reaction concerning most things is seldom based on logic. It is usually a matter of feeling—an intuitive feeling. You either like it or you don't. The logical reasons do not matter.

Pam and Tom will simply have to understand the basic natures of males and females. He needs to be aware of the fact that she *feels* her way to an answer whereas he lays the facts out in one-two-three order to reach a decision. She should not ask for his opinion unless she is prepared to accept his reasoning. Compassion for the feelings of one another will have to prevail before a solution can be reached.

CONCLUSION

1. Men and women are different physically and emotionally. There are also personality traits which cross the male-female lines. Conflicts are both inevitable and quite normal.

2. A happy marriage is not one that is free from conflict. Instead, it is one in which the partners have learned to resolve their differences with a minimum of hurt to one another.

3. Couples can often be more objective about their differences if they will only take the time to classify them (in writing) as important and unimportant.

4. Three general suggestions in learning to deal with differences are:
   (1) Tolerate
   (2) Rotate
   (3) Negotiate

5. Marital irritations can become explosive if they are not dealt with properly in the beginning stages.

SUGGESTIONS FOR CLASS DISCUSSION
Chapter 9

1. *Happily married couples have no conflicts.* Is this a fact or a myth?

2. Why do we usually have conflict with those we care about the most?

3. List all the differences which you have with your marriage partner. Put a star by the ones you consider to be important. Ask your mate to do the same. Compare lists. Which of these will you learn to live with and which of them demand change?

4. Discuss these methods of dealing with differences:
   (1) Tolerate
   (2) Rotate
   (3) Negotiate
   (Add to the list.)

5. Some examples of marital irritations were given in the lesson. With your husband or wife, compose your own list. Which ones will you tolerate? Which ones will you deal with by taking turns? By negotiations?

6. Discuss each of the case studies. What is the best solution in each?

7. Cite similar case studies depicting other areas of differences and conflicts.

8. Do you agree or disagree that most of the problems in marriage stem from conflicts arising over differences in individuals rather than actual sin?

WHEN THERE IS
NETWORK TROUBLE

10

A few years ago, the Family Services Association conducted a survey which revealed that eighty-seven percent of husbands and wives interviewed said that the number one problem in their marriages was communication. Though communication involves many topics and because problems revolve around several issues, the difficulties of communication in marriage related basically to the husband-wife relationship. Many people believe their problem is a lack of communication. Inasmuch as we communicate in so many ways, it is doubtful that this is the real problem. Instead, the real issue is their failure to understand their own emotional and psychological involvement in every issue that makes communication such a dynamic force for good or bad in the marriage relationship. There are several deeply hidden areas in each person's life that are of special importance. When any issue arises that touches one of these areas, there is an immediate psychological response. To the casual observer the issue itself is not that important but, because of the emotional involvement, it becomes a highly charged force to be dealt with. This is an important aspect of communication that few understand and therefore triggers many problems. Let's examine them.

EGO. Of all the problems of communication, this is the most common. It raises the question, "Am I important?" Though arguments may range over topics of money, time, energy, or other people, these are not the issues. The real issue is that one or both partners behave in such a way as to make the other feel that he or she doesn't rank very high on the spouse's list of priorities.

When a husband shows little regard for the time and effort his wife has invested in preparing a meal or gives more attention and time to his hunting dog and equipment than to his wife, they will argue about those matters. There will be no real communication, however, because often neither understands that this is not the real issue. The real issue is what he is saying about her importance to him. It is her ego that is at stake.

Wives create the same problems in the lives of their husbands. The amount of money lavished on the house or on the children often makes him feel that they are more important to her than he is. Though they may discuss these problems, rarely do they communicate about the real issue—whether or not he is really important to her. It appears to him that she views the house and children as being more valuable than he is. Often this part of the problem is especially difficult for her to grasp because she has been taught all her life that a good wife will be a good housekeeper, and a good mother will spend a lot of time with her children. To her he is acting childishly and selfishly. Whether he realizes it or not, his sense of self-worth has been challenged and it is a fight for survival for him.

POWER STRUGGLE. This issue involves decision making. In this marriage who calls the shots? Are all decisions the responsibility of the husband or does the wife share in the decision making, especially within clearly defined areas? Does she ever have the right to disagree with his decision and voice her own opinion on a matter?

The problem raised by a power struggle is not what a couple argues over; they argue over everything! He insists that he is right always and refuses to listen to her or even entertain the idea that he may be wrong. It is as if he were something more than human. The headship role of the husband as defined by God in Ephesians chapter 5 and 1 Peter chapter 3 does not make him infallible nor does it invalidate and exclude the wisdom, understanding, and ability of the wife. (A complete discussion of the subject of roles is found in the chapters "We're Different" and "Identity Conflicts—Which Am I?") Verse 21 of Ephesians 5 commands us to submit to one another in every relationship of life. The verses following make application of that principle to marriage. The third chapter of 1 Peter discusses marriage first and then broadens to all life's relationships as it admonishes us to "be ye all of one mind, having compassion one of another; love as brethren (Christians), be pitiful, be courteous" (verse 8). A Christian husband must never manipulate these verses in order to refuse to let his wife have an opinion, and a Christian wife must never view them in such a light as to be made to feel that her husband must be considered right even when she knows he is wrong. Though their roles are different, they are equals and must treat each other as such. The reality of the matter is that they are both human and, at times, both are wrong; but they must each be willing, at the very least, to explore the ideas of the other.

Why do power struggles create such problems? Why are there arguments over an endless stream of issues? Because this, too, involves ego. Each feels that giving in would be a blow to self-worth. That, however, is rarely what is discussed.

SPACE. In the feeling of individual worth, each person needs his or her own breathing room. The amount varies with each individual; but until a couple understands this principle and deals with it in a way satisfactory to both, it will be a source of constant friction. She may complain about not getting to be with him enough or about his lack of affection, while at the same time he accuses her of smothering him and complaining that she leaves him no time for himself or for hobbies. They need to communicate about the space needs of both and work toward a compromise they could both accept and live with. He must realize her need for cuddling and feeling close, and she must recognize that he needs time to devote to things other than to her alone. This opening and closing of space can work continually in such way as to help each appreciate the other more.

SEX. Several needs vary widely in individuals but sex plays an important role in every marriage. It is reserved exclusively for this relationship and is intended by God to be a source of deep joy and fulfillment. Instead of communicating directly with one another about expectations as to how often and under what circumstances and other relevant matters, couples often evade the issue by becoming exhausted through overwork either at home or at the office, by allowing the children's lifestyle to interfere, or by countless other excuses. These excuses often become the subject of conversation rather than the real issue. If they are trying to avoid each other and the fulfillment of their God-assigned roles, they need to face that problem and, through good communication, resolve it.

TERRITORIAL INVASION. A sense of territorial rights has a lot to do with our sense of identity, our ego, and our role in the marriage relationship. The woman of the house considers the house her territory. She is responsible in her own mind and in the eyes of society around her for how it is kept (God calls her the homekeeper: 1 Timothy 5:14; Titus 2:5). When others interfere through criticism or personal interference, she is hurt and angered. Regardless of what the ensuing discussion is about, the real problem is territorial invasion and that is where good communication is needed. The husband may have a workshop, a den, or even just a desk that he considers his own. Tamper here and you have invaded his territory and he will be quick to respond. He usually considers driving to be his territory and will resent his wife insisting on driving him or advising him as a backseat driver.

In the animal world various species mark and clearly define their territory. When another of the same species invades, there is an immediate war. We humans often are not smart enough to know that this is the real source of many of our problems. We discuss many issues it raises but rarely communicate our true feelings: "I'm hurt because you have invaded my territory and I'm fighting in order to hold on to what's mine!"

TRUST. No issue is more important to the happiness and stability of a marriage than mutual trust. Among the attitudes Paul declared to be necessary in the life of every Christian is the one that states, "Love . . . thinketh no evil" (1 Corinthians 13:5). In the language of everyday living it says, "I trust you completely." If one or both partners of the marriage feel threatened by the vulnerability of complete openness, that door will quickly be closed. How many issues are discussed and how many problems are fought over when the real culprit is lack of trust! When we can communicate about trust and work toward building trust, many problems will solve themselves.

ROLE FULFILLMENT. This does not refer to the matter of subjection, leadership, and related subjects per se but to the issue of self-identity. So often a facade is built, especially in the presence of those whom we wish to impress, thus hiding the real personality. Sooner or later the time comes when that facade must come down, and we must live our lives as the real people we are. When unreal expectations are made of us, whether through our own misleading or some other cause, our inner self rebels by saying, "That is not the real me." Real communication enables both partners to see the true role of the other and allows them to fulfill that role. Putting the other in a role foreign or unnatural is a real cause for dispute. From the earliest of our association with one another, each should simply be himself or herself. To appear to be what you are not sets you up for unreal expectations from your partner later on.

Because we often communicate without understanding the real issues, isn't it almost a foregone conclusion that much of our communication will be bad instead of good? We do indeed have network trouble. We may think we talk about facts and ideas. That is usually satisfying to a man because that's his basic interest; but, for a woman, real communication means discussing feelings. She wants to talk about how she feels about things and, just as importantly, wants to know and understand her husband's feelings. Again, we encounter a barrier to good communication because, unlike his wife, he does not relate well to feelings. He often doesn't know how he feels himself; how can he tell her? So we are back to square one again. We communicate but do it badly and the marriage suffers.

Since eighty-seven percent of the couples polled said communication was the number one problem in their marriage, what were the major issues in their communication problem? As they perceived them, they are the items discussed in the remainder of this chapter. I think you will find them universal in bad communication.

LOADED WORDS. Though they are different with every individual and with each marriage, there are certain words that are so loaded with explosive power that the use of them brings an immediate hurt. We resort to the use of them when we want to fight dirty and win an immediate victory. The angry reaction which they bring, however, can last a long time. A friend of mine tells of the time he called his slightly overweight wife "Pudge" for the last time. When we make fun of a person's weakness, shortcoming, or physical defects, we are using loaded words.

To distort truth by making statements like *you always* or *you never* or *all you ever* is also to use loaded words. There are no such absolutes, so to make it appear that such action is *always* or *never* true of a person is obviously a bad way to try to communicate. You are communicating but nothing positive can come from that kind of communication.

Words are powerful. Words that hurt do great damage. Solomon tells us: "Death and life are in the power of the tongue" (Proverbs 18:21). James warns us that the tongue can become "an unruly evil, full of deadly poison" (James 3:8).

EMOTIONAL LANGUAGE. Communication can be both verbal and nonverbal. Emotional language is both. When emotions are allowed to control communication, we usually quit dealing with the real issues and begin attacking the other's ego and self-identity. Not all emotional language is wrong. Crying when hurt is inevitable for some, but to use crying as a means of dominating another person or prematurely ending a discussion is wrong. In the same way, voice tones and facial expressions can be natural responses or they could be dramatics used to control the conversation.

Disagreements are inevitable and we are all by nature emotional beings. However, when we resort to emotional language as a means of communication, a discussion quickly degenerates into a quarrel. The Word of God condemns quarreling: "Let all bitterness, and wrath, and anger, and clamor, and evil speaking, be put away from you, with all malice" (Ephesians 4:31); "As coals are to burning coals, and wood to fire; so is a contentious man to kindle strife" (Proverbs 26:21).

FAULTFINDING WORDS. Someone has defined the faultfinder as "that old buzzard that soars over the landscape of human relations looking for something rotten." All of us have faults and anyone who looks for them can find them. The difference between the humming bird that sips nectar and the buzzard that eats carrion is that each finds what it is looking for. Unlike constructive criticism given in love, faultfinding is destructive. The purpose of this kind of communication is to tear down the other person and lower self-esteem by attacking the ego. The problem is never solved by communicating in this way; it is always enlarged. Christians are taught to encourage one another (1 Thessalonians 5:14). Paul exhorts us: "Let us not therefore judge one another any more: but judge this rather, that no man put a stumblingblock or an occasion to fall in his brother's way" (Romans 14:13).

BACKHANDED COMPLIMENTS. This is a poorly disguised way of faultfinding. Rather than a direct frontal approach, a cowardly route is taken. The point being made is obvious, but there is always a back door left open so the critic can deny that was his intent or insist that the words be taken literally and at face value. James tells us: "Let your yea be yea; and your nay, nay" (James 5:12). Jesus teaches, "Let your communication be Yea, yea; Nay, nay: for whatsoever is more than these cometh of evil" (Matthew 5:37). When we intend to mean something other than what we actually say, we are courting danger. When the verbal and nonverbal behavior do not match, we are simply lying in one form of communication or the other. Christians are to "speak the truth in love" (Ephesians 4:15) and "putting away lying, speak every man truth with his neighbor" (verse 25). It does no good to say one thing and then complain, "You should have known what I meant!"

Sometimes we reverse this method by asking a question that seeks a different answer than that made obvious by the question. We are fishing for a compliment without the courage to ask for it. When a direct answer is given to the question, we become offended. No question should be asked unless we are willing to accept an honest answer. Good communication demands that couples be able to speak honestly and openly to each other.

EXCUSE MAKING. Almost every form of communication elicits some kind of response. When we are criticized, our normal response is a countercriticism which we feel makes things even. When someone complains, we answer with a countercomplaint and feel justified. When the criticism is deserved and the complaint is real, our excuse making shows our lack of sensitivity to the hurts and needs of the other. It is a counterattack at a time when that person is most vulnerable.

Very common to this kind of communication is when someone brings up a present failure and we counter with some past failure on his or her part. It makes no sense, of course, and never solves the problem. This is the reason that some couples can turn a short, simple discussion of some issue into hours of quarreling. Every past mistake on the part of either is dug up and rehashed. For couples who communicate in this way, the longer their relationship has lasted the longer the argument lasts, because they have just that much more to argue about. Jesus' parable of the talents (Matthew 25:14-30) illustrates the futility of excuse making. Solomon said, "He that regardeth reproof shall be honored" (Proverbs 13:18).

IDLE WORDS. Many people have a bad habit of putting their mouths into action before their brains are in gear. Such a person has a bad case of "foot-and-mouth disease." Their speech is usually impulsive and very often they say things that shouldn't have been said and wouldn't have been said if they had taken a moment to think about it. On the other hand they often find it easy to excuse themselves with a flippant: "You know me; I just say things like that. I don't really mean it." All words are important and even words thoughtlessly spoken can wound deeply. Rather than dismiss such a shortcoming lightly, remember the teaching of the Bible: "Let every man be . . . slow to speak" (James 1:19); "Whoso keepeth his mouth and his tongue, keepeth his soul from troubles" (Proverbs 21:23); "Seest thou a man that is hasty in his words? There is more hope of a fool than of him" (Proverbs 29:20).

INCESSANT TALK. There are many reasons for some people to talk too much. Regardless of the reason, excessive talk is poor communication. If we feel that we are insecure, that we are not getting through to others, that we are not being heard, we often compensate by talking too much. Incessant talk is also a means of controlling the conversation of the other person involved.

Such excessive talking often takes on the form of nagging. Nagging is one of the most common complaints in troubled marriages. Though it is a form of communication, it has very little positive value. That's not to say it doesn't accomplish anything. It produces quarrels, resentment, and turning a deaf ear. The scriptures warn us against incessant talk: "In the multitude of words there wanteth not sin: but he that refraineth his lips is wise" (Proverbs 10:19). Those who speak much have much for which to be responsible: "For by thy words thou shalt be justified, and by thy words thou shalt be condemned" (Matthew 12:37).

SILENCE. While it is possible to convey acceptance and other important things by silence, it is usually a means of pouting, ignoring, or sulking, A refusal to commit oneself to words creates doubt and confusion. Often it is a very destructive weapon called *the silent treatment.* Some people are just quieter by nature than others; they are more contemplative than expressive. Don't make more of that kind of silence than is necessary.

Though silence is an absence of words, it is still a powerful means of communication. In fact, nonverbal communication (it has many forms) bears a heavier burden of expressing a message than words and voice tones combined. Respect it as a powerful tool and use it wisely. To use it exclusively is to ignore the advice of the Bible when it says: "There is . . . a time to keep silence and a time to speak" (Ecclesiastes 3:7).

Two other forms of nonverbal communication which are often misused are refusing to *look* and to *listen*. At home we often have to talk to each other from one room to another, while engaged in other activities, often even with our backs turned to the one with whom we are conversing. In serious communication, we must take time to pay attention and really listen to what is being said. When we won't do this, we are making a pointed message that says, "I'm not interested" or "You are not that important to me." Wandering eyes speak loudly of lack of interest.

The fact that we are not listening is shown by facial expressions, impatient looks, sighs, drumming the fingers. Such actions speak volumes. On the other hand, when we listen with rapt attention we are saying: "You are important. I am interested in you and I respect what you have to say." God's Word admonishes us to be good listeners (James 1:19).

CONCLUSION

Having seen the many ways we fail to understand the real issues involved in meaningful communication and having examined some of the ways we communicate very badly, let's close this chapter with a look at five ways we can improve family communication.

1. Learn to express how you feel honestly but with warmth and understanding, knowing that your feelings are not the only ones involved.

2. Learn how to express your feelings of anger or irritation by directing them at the issue rather than the person. Avoid making *you* statements.

3. Learn that very sensitive issues can best be discussed after anger and irritation have cooled off.

4. Learn the importance of *I feel* statements. How you feel about a matter is more important and closer to truth than dogmatic statements about issues.

5. Learn to avoid saying, "I told you so." There are many ways of saying this, both verbally and nonverbally. Avoid saying it in any way.

SUGGESTIONS FOR CLASS DISCUSSION
Chapter 10

1. What is generally considered to be the number one problem in most marriages?

2. Discuss this statement from the text: "The real problem is their failure to understand their own emotional and psychological involvement in every issue that makes communication such a dynamic force for good or bad in the marriage relationship."

3. Couples may argue over the time and money the husband spends on hunting or over the time and money which she invests in the furnishings of the house or on the children. What is the real issue underlying these arguments? Can the disputes be resolved until the issues are recognized?

4. How can a power struggle precipitate disagreements? Does a woman's role of subjection make her inferior? Ephesians 5:21 commands us to submit to one another. Discuss this principle in the overall role of subjection.

5. How do men and women differ in their needs for space? How can a lack of understanding be the cause of conflict?

6. God reserved sexual fulfillment exclusively for the marriage relationship. What are some causes of conflict? How can they be resolved?

7. What does a woman generally consider to be her territorial rights? What are some areas which a man usually claims?

How does an invasion of one another's territory cause conflict?

8. First Corinthians 13:5 stresses trust. How can a lack of trust prevent honest communication?

9. Sometimes a husband or wife is forced into an unnatural role due to the expectations of the other. For example, a wife may want her husband to bare his deepest feelings on a subject. A man's natural thought processes revolve around logic and reasoning, not emotions. She is expecting him to assume a role which feels uncomfortable to him. A wife may be forced into the role of providing a living for the family and feel resentment. What are the implications of role fulfillment in the marriage relationship?

10. Cite some examples of *loaded words*. Relate the passages found in Proverbs 18:21 and James 3:8 to this problem.

11. Emotional language can be both verbal and nonverbal. What can tears, voice tones, and facial expressions convey?

12. Faultfinding words attack another's ego. Naturally a person will fight for survival. Give examples of some faultfinding words. How does this relate to open communication in expressing how we honestly feel?

13. What are some *backhanded* compliments?

14. Excuse making is a deterrent to good communication. For example, a mate may bring up a present failure. The husband or wife may countercharge with a past failure on the part of the other. What is the solution?

15. Relate these passages to the problem of idle words:
    James 1:19
    Proverbs 21:23
    Proverbs 29:20

16. How can incessant talk damage a marriage? (Note Proverbs 10:19 and Matthew 12:37).

17. Silence is a form of nonverbal communication. Is it good or bad? What is the principle involved in Ecclesiastes 3:7?

18. When one partner refuses to look and to listen, what is the message generally transmitted to the other?

19. At the conclusion of this chapter are found five ways in which family communication can be improved. Discuss these in class.

WHEN "I DO"
BECOMES "I DON'T"

11

Marriage is a lifelong commitment. The vows made are not to be taken lightly. On this issue the Bible gives no ground. The line is clearly drawn and no one is allowed any evasion of responsibility. The rules are rigid and will not bend.

God speaks gravely concerning the making of vows:

> If a man shall vow a vow unto the Lord, or swear an oath to bind his soul with a bond; he shall not break his word, he shall do according to all that proceedeth out of his mouth (Numbers 30:2).

> When thou vowest a vow unto God, defer not to pay it: for he hath no pleasure in fools: pay that which thou hast vowed. Better is it that thou shouldest not vow, than that thou shouldest vow and not pay. Suffer not thy mouth to cause thy flesh to sin; neither say thou before the angel, that it was an error: Wherefore should God be angry at thy voice, and destroy the work of thine hands (Ecclesiastes 5:4-6).

Once the vow has been made and *the point of no return* has been passed, it is sin to say, "It was an error." How many times do people convince themselves after the wedding, perhaps even several years later, that it was all a mistake. Either they should never have married or they should not have married the one whom they did. All such reasoning is vain. Once a little boy returned home from Sunday School but, instead of enjoying the usual Sunday dinner, he went directly to bed. His mother asked if he were sick and he said he had a pain in his side. The Sunday School lesson that morning was about how God made Eve by taking a rib from Adam's side. The little boy exclaimed, "I'm afraid I'm about to get a wife and I'm not ready for one yet!" A lot of men get a wife when they are not ready for one yet, but this is one area where God makes no provision for a change of mind. Marriage is a lifelong commitment.

In many different ways Israel had tried the patience of God. They had broken every command He had given. They had violated the sacred covenant they had made with Jehovah. Yet they regarded such contempt of the sacred lightly. Often they even argued with God about the matter. They could see nothing wrong with what they were doing. A case in point is found in Malachi chapter two. As a nation they had ignored their marriage vows. When God confronted them with their sin and spoke of how weary He was with their continued disobedience, their reply was: "Wherein have we wearied him?" (verse 17). They had actually become so brazen in their sin that the verse continues by saying, "Everyone that doeth evil is good in the sight of the Lord, and he delighteth in them." Indeed, "Wherein have we wearied him?"

Notice the sequence of events:

1. They had covered the altar of the Lord with tears, with weeping, and with crying out (verse 13).

2. He regarded not their offering any more (verse 13).

3. They had the gall to ask "Why?" (verse 14).

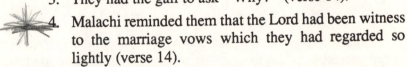
4. Malachi reminded them that the Lord had been witness to the marriage vows which they had regarded so lightly (verse 14).

5. They had been married a long time and were abandoning the wives of their youth (verse 14).

6. Their actions in this matter were contrary to the sacred covenant (verse 14).

7. Their actions against their wives were considered treacherous (verse 15).

8. They attempted to cover their violence (verse 16).

9. The conclusion: "For the Lord, the God of Israel, saith that he hateth putting away" (verse 16). Could God let this facade continue? "Where is the God of judgment?" (verse 17).

This lifelong commitment is not only in regard to maintaining the marriage but also means absolute faithfulness. God's Word gives no ground on this issue either. There must be total fidelity on the part of both husband and wife. Adultery is strictly forbidden by God. He commanded Israel, "Thou shalt not commit adultery" (Exodus 20:14). Jesus reminded the rich young ruler that this was God's standard (Matthew 19:18). When Paul wrote to the churches of Galatia, he warned them against the works of the flesh, reminding them that those guilty could not go to heaven. Adultery was specified (Galatians 5:19).

The faithfulness we vow to each other on our wedding day does not depend on happiness, success, fulfillment, or any other factor. Of course that makes little sense to a sin-jaded world; but in God's original creation, it made perfect sense both to God and to Adam and Eve. It is rumored that on one occasion Eve said to Adam, "Am I your one and only love?" to which he replied, "Who else?" That is still God's will and the only arrangement He will accept. It is also the only way for men and women to find heaven's happiness on this earth.

So important is this sexual commitment that God has decreed that for the sin of breaking this vow and for this sin only may the marriage itself be dissolved. In Matthew 19:1-9 Jesus explained that God's original intention was that no exception would be made at all. Once the marriage took place, it would end only by the death of one of the partners. After sin entered the world the picture changed. Now there is one exception. When one's mate is guilty of adultery, the innocent party has the right to dissolve the marriage and seek a new marriage with someone else. Even here one party has committed grievous sin. If done under any other circumstance, both parties are guilty of sin. Sexual purity is demanded of all who would be acceptable to God.

Some confuse the courthouse and its human laws with the God of heaven and His sacred decree. Others accept the norm of the age while many answer only to their own whims and fancies. Remember, it is the Word of God by which our actions are judged right or wrong (John 12:48). That must be the guiding word and the final word in our commitment of marriage to our lifelong mate.

There is an old story about a community which received its water supply from a spring high on a mountain overlooking the hamlet. On that mountain lived an old man who was paid a small sum by the villagers to keep the limbs and leaves and other debris out of the stream. One day, in an effort to cut expenses, the town council voted to dispense with the old man's services. After all, they reasoned, the money he received was more of a gift than a salary anyway. They viewed the job itself as quite unnecessary. Then illness struck the village. One by one they fell prey to disease until it became epidemic. What was the source of the illness? They discovered that their water was contaminated. Without the services of the old man to keep the spring, what had been pure and wholesome became the source of contamination. Quickly they put the old man back to work and soon the stream was clean again. Good health was restored to the village. Marriage after the ordinance of God is *the keeper of the spring*. His laws keep it pure and holy. Disregard those sacred ordinances and marriage itself can become a source of pollution. All kinds of social and spiritual disease can break out. Today's world has dismissed *the keeper of the spring* as outdated and unneeded. And even *wise* men wonder what strange illness grips mankind. Look around you. Don't you see how desperately we need *the keeper of the spring*?

WHEN COMMITMENT DIES

Often the *I do* becomes *I don't*, not in the form of a divorce or a formal breakup of the home but in the dying of commitment. While it is true that the commitment of marriage is a once-for-all declaration made at the time of the wedding, the declaration of that commitment should be made repeatedly. That repetition fills a deep need of our humanity. Akio Limb tells of being asked years ago by his wife, Charlene, "Akio, do you love me?" In the stoicism characteristic of the Far East he replied, "I told you I loved you when I married you. If I change my mind I'll let you know." Somehow that is not enough for most of us. We need the reassurance that is given by the restating of our commitment. Those coming to the marriage altar must understand they are making a commitment. The years of marriage following the wedding need to be marked by the reaffirmation of those vows. On each anniversary of that wedding, couples might like to repeat vows to each other similar to the ones made on their wedding day: "You and you only, for better or for worse, in sickness and in health, in adversity and in prosperity, until we are parted by death." Perhaps you could turn to 1 Corinthians 13 and rephrase Paul's discourse on love:

> I vow to you again a love that is patient, kind, and enduring. I give you a life that is not jealous or possessive or proud or selfish or rude or inconsiderate. My love for you will not insist on its own way, nor will it be irritable, resentful, or keep an account of wrongs and failures. It will rejoice when good prevails. It is a love that knows no limit to its endurance, no end to its trust, and no fading of its hope. My love for you will outlast everything else and will stand when everything else has failed. For our future years I hold faith, hope, and love; but the greatest of these is love.

Sometimes the lack of commitment, both to the spouse and to the marriage, is not a matter of the lack of words about commitment. With some, words come easily. While words are very important, they are not sufficient by themselves. Our lips may be saying "I'm committed," but our deeds may be denying it. Two of the leading indicators of commitment are time and money. Inasmuch as "where your treasure is, there will your heart be also" (Luke 12:34), if we will look carefully at the investment of the time and money in our lives, we will see what is truly important to us. There lies our commitment.

Time is not only a great treasure; it is a great equalizer. For each of us there is the same amount of time in each day, week, month, and year. For the young and the old, educated and uneducated, rich and poor, garbage collector and president of the United States, there is no difference. For each there are 168 hours in each week. How you use them reveals your commitment. Some of the hours are demanded for work, eating, and sleeping. Some are given to education, recreation, and other worthwhile choices. Among the many choices that confront us, to which do we give the most hours of our week? Findings indicate that at the bottom of the list is the time devoted to marriage maintenance: between one and two percent of those 168 hours. Many give far more time to the lawn, to entertaining friends, or to talking to casual acquaintances than they do to the actual work of maintaining their marriages! It is no wonder we have lost our commitment!

If most were asked, "How much time do you spend with your wife or husband?" the answer would be, "Lots. We eat together, sleep together, watch TV together." That is not the kind of time investment needed to maintain the marriage commitment. It must be quality time. Often the kind of time that is spent together is of such nature that neither of the two is hardly aware of the presence of the other. There must be time for sharing ideas and ideals, time for real communication. Often this kind of time is so unimportant to us that we let a casual telephone conversation with someone else usurp its place. Examine your life and see where the actual allotment of time, money, and energy goes. By seeing realistically where we spend these resources, we can fairly accurately determine both what we are committed to and also the degree or depth of that commitment.

Is there money in your marriage for hobbies, clothes, houses and countless other things, but no money for a vacation together each year, just the two of you? Is there no money for a date and dinner on a regular basis, just the two of you? If not, it is because of a lack of commitment to the maintenance of your marriage. When money is available for everything else in life but none available, or at least none ever allocated and used in ways for just the two of you to share without interruption, you can be sure you need some serious work on priorities. We say that next to our commitment to God comes our commitment to our marriage. But does it show? How could any couple so sorely neglect such a vital part of their lives?

In the maintenance of our marriage, as is true with so many other things, regularity is the key. With so many it is neglected until serious trouble arises, then some serious attention and work until the crisis passes. Then it is back to neglect again. Marriage cannot live on famine and feast. A quick vacation does not automatically solve the problems created by months of neglect. Plan regular times for togetherness and keep those plans. Let nothing but an emergency of the highest order cause you to break the plans. Whatever causes the plans to be broken is often seen to be more important to your partner than the plans and perhaps even the marriage itself.

Commitment is the voluntary taking of obligation and responsibility. In the case of marriage it is sacred responsibility. Never, in any sense, let your *I do* become *I don't*. The fate of our society and of your soul depends upon your honoring that vow of obligation.

IN A NUTSHELL

1. The making of a vow before God is a very serious matter. Once the marriage vows have been taken, those involved have reached *the point of no return*. Death is the only honorable way that the union can be severed.

2. Absolute sexual faithfulness is demanded by God. Unfaithfulness is the only sin for which the marriage can be dissolved.

3. All too often a marriage suffers from the dying of commitment. The vows should be constantly reinforced by both
   word and deed.

4. Two of the most important indicators of commitment are
   time and money. A wise husband and wife will invest a
   generous amount of both in their marriage.

SUGGESTIONS FOR CLASS DISCUSSION
Chapter 11

1. Centuries ago God spoke of the seriousness of vows in
   Numbers 30:2 and Ecclesiastes 5:4-6. Read these two passages aloud in class and comment.

2. What is *the point of no return* in the marriage vows?

3. In the second chapter of Malachi, examine verses 13-17
   and note the sequence of events. Why was God not regarding their offering any longer?

4. What is strictly forbidden in these passages: Exodus
   20:14; Matthew 19:18; Galatians 5:19?

5. Does faithfulness to marriage vows depend upon happiness?

6. According to Matthew 19:1-9, what was God's original
   intention for marriage? After sin entered the world, what
   was the one exception?

7. When the laws of the land and the Word of God are in
   conflict, which must be obeyed? Note John 12:48.

8. Discuss the illustration of "The Keeper of the Spring"
   regarding the importance of keeping marriage pure at its
   source.

9. What is the value of repeated commitment of the marriage
   vows?

10. Distinguish between commitment to the spouse and com-
    mitment to the marriage vows. Which is more important?

EXERCISES

Two of the leading indicators of commitment are time and money. Tabulate the amount of each which you and your mate devote to marriage maintenance by filling in the exercise below.

Amount of time spent with one another discussing feelings on a daily basis:

Sunday   _____

Monday   _____

Tuesday   _____

Wednesday   _____

Thursday   _____

Friday   _____

Saturday   _____

_____ Number of times you spent with one another this week in a recreational activity

_____ Number of times you spent with each other in a shared work project this week

_____ Number of times this month that just the two of you dined out at some special place

_____ Number of times during the past six months that you and your spouse spent a weekend, or even a night, away from the rest of the family

_____ Number of times during the past year that you or your mate surprised one another with a gift for no special occasion

Look over your responses. If time and money are fairly accurate indications of commitment to any cause, how dedicated are you to your marriage?

WHEN "I WILL"
BECOMES "I WON'T"

12

The key that unlocks the secret of happy lives together is Ephesians 5:21 in which Paul lays down the principle that in every relationship there is a mutual submission: "Submitting yourselves one to another in the fear of God." It involves a recognition of full equality and respect for each other and an overriding desire on the part of each to please the other. It is pictured as two yoked together, sharing a common burden, and pulling a mutual load. Unless each is willing to do his or her share, the load could be handled much easier without the other. Without help, one must pull not only the load, but the unwilling partner in the yoke as well.

In the work of the church, for example, believers are yoked together with a common burden. In his discussion of the distribution of gifts necessary to the accomplishing of that task, Paul is careful to explain that each must do his own part (1 Corinthians chapters 12 and 13). The reason? Neither can say to the other, "I have no need of you" (12:21); but "that the members should have the same care one for another" (12:25). In Ephesians chapter 4 he says, "The whole body fitly joined together and compacted by that which every joint supplieth, according to the effectual working in the measure of every part" (verse 16). That is mutual ministry made possible by mutual submission. Nothing else can work. In Colossians 2:2,19 he mentions how this *knits* us together. You know what happens when the knitting is not properly done; it unravels into a useless mess.

The same principle applies in the home because the relationship is a type of the relationship in the church (Ephesians 5:32). Here, also, one cannot say to the other, "I have no need of you." Here, too, we "should have the same care one for another," "be fitly joined together and compacted by that which every joint supplieth, according to the effectual working in the measure of every part," and be "knit together in love."

Mutual submission means that a wife has no right to view herself as a maid because of her normal household responsibilities. Nor is she to consider these tasks as below her dignity or demeaning to her ability and standing. Once a husband was darning a pair of socks as he and his wife carried on a running battle of words. "Since you don't do this," he said, "I have to do it myself." She replied, "You think you can do everything better than I can anyway, so go ahead." His response was, "I may not do it perfectly but I do know how to do it." As the battle continued she said, "Know how to do it! Why you don't even know which finger the thimble belongs on." He replied, "That I *do* know! It belongs on *your* finger!" Such a battle of words is not all that uncommon in many households, but it does not fit God's picture of mutual submission.

Such mutual submission also means the husband has no right to view the home as his castle and the wife as his slave. Many men tend to think of themselves in the home as the well-known E. F. Hutton. That means, "When he speaks, everybody listens."

Every Christian is admonished: "Bear ye one another's burdens" (Galatians 6:2). Since that is true of every Christian relationship, how much more is it true of the relationship between a husband and a wife. Yet too many have the attitude that one hiker had when he and his companion saw a bear coming down the same trail on the mountainside they had just descended. He sat down and quickly removed his boots, replacing them with a pair of running shoes. "Surely," his companion said, "you don't think you can outrun that bear!" "I don't have to" was his reply. "I only have to outrun you." Too many marriages suffer because one partner runs away from responsibility, leaving the other to face it alone.

In the words of the song made famous by Hank Williams, Jr., we all need an "attitude adjustment." Perhaps nothing as drastic as a knock on the head and a kick on the shin and a couple of bites by Rin Tin Tin, but something needs to get our attention enough to allow us to see how badly wrong attitudes can affect a marriage. The answer is in Paul's admonition: "Let this mind be in you, which was also in Christ Jesus" (Philippians 2:5). That mind is the mind of a servant. When, at the Last Supper, the disciples disputed about which of them would be greatest, He reminded them that true greatness comes not from having the most authority but from being the best servant (Luke 22:24-27). The greatest husband or wife is the one who serves the other best.

When and where did the beautiful attitude of submission lose its meaning? When a famous heart surgeon submits himself to the wisdom and safekeeping of an airplane pilot, is he demeaning himself? If that same pilot submits himself to the wisdom and safekeeping of that surgeon for open-heart surgery, is that belittling? Then why should we consider the mutual submission relationships of life (Ephesians 5:21), and especially those of marriage, to be dishonoring?

Perhaps customs and traditions of the past, which were completely acceptable for that day, have been perpetuated beyond their age and can no longer be accepted, so we have thrown the principle away along with the tradition. I grew up in a generation of educated and trained men who were expected to make all decisions. Today's women are as educated and well-trained as men and far more capable of helping to make major decisions than were their counterparts of past generations. Why should a tradition be honored when it no longer serves a useful function? Several years ago a friend of mine died and left behind a middle-aged wife who had never made a bank deposit, written a check, paid a bill, dealt with a utility company, called a plumber or an electrician, or countless other things now so necessary to her life. She was left virtually helpless with no decision-making skills whatever. What they both had accepted as traditionally right was a great injustice.

Often the distaste for the word *submission* springs from the action of a tyrant like the ruler in THE KING AND I. His word in everything was law with no questions, no *ifs, and*s, or *but*s. Such an arrangement is deplorable and both partners are to be pitied. Something has gone terribly wrong in the lives of both.

While roles as given by God never change, customs and traditions do. Mutual submission is a Bible principle and absolutely necessary to the functioning of society. As it applies to the family, it means "decision making shared in cooperation." Obviously there are minor decisions that each partner must constantly make alone. To require every decision to be discussed or to demand that every decision first be okayed by your partner would so bog down the system that it simply could not operate at all. Some decisions should not be made without seeking the advice and the counsel of your mate, but even then you must make the final decision. All truly big and important decisions must be made cooperatively. Even here the scale ought to tilt in favor of the one who has the greatest wisdom and experience in that area. And no decision ought ever be made that is purely selfish. Submission means that in each decision the one who makes it is doing what is best for the marriage. When this attitude is not present, sin is and the marriage will suffer.

To achieve the happiness God intended marriage to bring, perhaps you need to make some changes in your marriage. Does that thought bring fright or delight? The older we get, the harder change is to accomplish. Sometimes it seems easier to live with the problem than to face the prospect of change. But, when needed, that change can bring joy and delight and put zest and excitement back into a tired relationship. Forget the old cliche, "You can't teach an old dog new tricks," and launch out boldly on a new course of action.

In keeping with the principle of mutual submission, try the following suggestions for change.

1. Inasmuch as there is room for change in all of us, make the first change in that over which you have control—your own life. This kind of change is the most impelling force for change in the life of your partner. There

is a law built into our universe that says we reap what we sow (Galatians 6:6-10). We often call it the *boomerang principle*. It is not ironclad but it is nearly always true. Smile and get a smile in return. Wave and someone waves back. That's true even among strangers. How much more true is this among those closest to us. Instead of demanding change or making a big demonstration over your plights, try modeling in your own life those qualities you would like to see in your spouse. It is amazing to see the growth in that direction.

2. Don't scare your husband or wife to death by suddenly becoming an entirely new person overnight. And don't expect that kind of change in your mate. Instead, work gradually toward a goal, making small steps upward.

3. Make the desire for change reasonable and measurable. Don't expect the unreasonable of yourself or your spouse. That's expecting more than God expects (Romans 12:1). And don't expect what cannot be measured. If there is some goal desired but you have no way of measuring, how would you ever know whether or not it has been reached?

When we were children my sister's favorite radio program was *Let's Pretend*. I didn't care for it. It's not that I didn't pretend—all children do. But I had rather pretend with *Superman* or *The Green Hornet* or *Sergeant Preston of the Yukon* than with the fairy tales of her program. In many ways when we grow up we fail to put away our childhood games. For many, marriage is just another *Let's Pretend*. It need not be so. It can be everything it ought to be but only if we follow God's plan. God's plan calls for the beautiful principle of mutual submission. The husband's role is leader. The wife has the role of manager. Their relationship is that of "submitting yourselves to one another in love" (Ephesians 5:21). Don't ever destroy that by letting "I will" become "I won't."

WHAT HAVE WE LEARNED?

1. Everybody is building and every building has some kind of foundation. There are no exceptions.

2. The true foundation for all building is respect for and obedience to the authority of God.

3. Materialism in any form is a poor foundation for building anything.

4. The number one cause of crashes of small aircraft is overloading. It is also a major cause of marriage failure.

5. In spite of the plain teaching of God's word on the subject, money is still a major source of conflict among people in today's world.

6. Money is necessary in this life so we need to learn proper guidelines for managing it.

7. Many myths about marriage are given much credence. We must cut through these myths and find solid ground for marriage.

SUGGESTIONS FOR CLASS DISCUSSION
Chapter 12

1. Discuss the chapter entitled "How to Lead by Following," noting God's original plan for different roles.

2. Ephesians 5:21 admonishes husbands and wives to submit to one another. How is this compatible with the remainder of the chapter, which teaches the subjection of a wife to her husband?

3. Relate Ephesians 4:16 both to the work of the church and to the marriage relationship. Are the members inferior to the elders? In what manner are the elders in submission to the members? Why must someone be given the leadership role?

4. When the wife reigns as queen in the home, how is she treated? What is her attitude toward her husband? What is her husband's attitude?

5. What can be done when a woman is married to a man who is domineering and totally insensitive to his wife's feelings?

6. When a husband abandons his leadership role (or never assumes it) and leaves all the decisions to his wife, how can the situation be improved?

7. Relate the principle of mutual submission to two professionals who willingly submit to one another when services are needed.

8. What customs and traditions of the past chained most women? What is the situation today?

9. Why does God's principle for roles never change?

10. Discuss the definition of mutual submission as it given in the text: "Decision making shared in cooperation."

11. If you want to see your mate change in some area, where should the first change originate? Give some examples of the *boomerang principle* in everyday situations.

12. Discuss the advantages of gradual change.

13. Why should change be measurable?

EXERCISE

No one can argue with success. Make an informal survey of couples who have accepted God's divine plan for roles and are happy in their marriages. Ask them these questions and then relate the answers to the class.

1. Did you begin your marriage with your present acceptance of roles or did you develop these attitudes with the passing of time?

2. Describe your role as you see it now.

3. Was your husband ever overbearing? How did you get him to become more considerate of your needs?

4. Did your wife ever tend to dominate you? How did you handle the situation?

5. How did you learn each other's needs in order that you might submit to one another?

6. When you feel that your mate has taken unfair advantage of you, what do you do?

7. What are the five most important lessons that you have learned about proper role fulfillment which you would be willing to pass on to others?

WHEN EMOTIONS CONTROL

13

The underlying cause for the breakup of most marriages can be traced to negative emotions. Envy, bragging, rude behavior, selfishness, rage, harboring grudges, and faultfinding are manifestations of twisted thinking.

In a previous chapter the word *emotions* was defined as a person's feelings based upon his *perception* of an event or circumstances—not the facts.

For example, Sam may be consumed with a problem connected with his work. His preoccupation with the situation may produce a detachment, an aloofness with Susan, his wife. She senses that a wall is slowly building up between them. A lack of communication prevents his telling her what is bothering him. Her emotions run wild and she honestly believes that he no longer loves her. The truth of the matter is that Sam adores Susan. Her emotions of fear, rage, and envy are not based upon facts. They are the result of her perception of the facts.

Negative emotions eat away at the mind and body as an acid, resulting in emotionally handicapped individuals and broken marriages. Most people have enough common sense to reach for some sort of antacid when there is a physical burning in the stomach but too often completely ignore the causes of negative emotions.

One very significant fact should be remembered. *No one can create an emotion within me. I produce my own emotions by my thoughts—both good and bad.* If I learn to monitor my thoughts, then I can begin to learn to control my emotions. "Whatsoever a man soweth, that shall he also reap" (Galatians 6:7). When I sow negative thoughts, I will inevitably experience negative emotions. "For as he thinketh in his heart, so is he" (Proverbs 23:7). "He that hath no rule over his own spirit is like a city that is broken down, and without walls" (Proverbs 25:28).

Everyone constantly talks to himself. Each waking minute is largely consumed with internal self-talk.

"He didn't speak to me. I'm angry."

"That was such a thoughtful gesture. I feel good."

"I really put my foot in my mouth that time. I always say the wrong thing."

"Say, you did a pretty good job!"

Practically every minute of the day we are feeding thoughts into the subconscious mind. That part of the brain has no way of distinguishing truth from error. It only accepts what is fed to it and reacts accordingly. In Acts 26:9 Paul expressed the same idea when he penned, "I verily thought with myself . . ."

Negative thoughts should be banned from the mind not only for the good of a marriage but also for one's personal well-being, including physical health. The impact of the emotions upon the body is profound. Emotions can produce a change in the rate of heartbeat. Blood pressure is also influenced. Feelings trigger contractions in the stomach and intestines. The entire glandular system is also controlled by emotions. Everyone who has ever experienced the fright of public speaking probably has felt the accompanying dry mouth. Overactive sweat glands cause clammy palms. The adrenal gland produces a surge of extra energy when it believes the body needs it for fight or flight. For example, some pranksters could prop up the head of a dead snake in the road. A person passing by could easily *believe* that he was about to be struck by the coiled snake. That perception would trigger the adrenal gland to produce sufficient adrenalin to enable a very hasty flight!

SUGGESTIONS FOR DEALING
WITH NEGATIVE EMOTIONS

Since negative emotions are harmful to the well-being of a marriage (to say nothing of the havoc they can cause to spiritual life, emotional outlook, and physical health), it is necessary to rid ourselves of them before they can be too destructive.

1. Do not remain in ignorance. Search God's Word. Study recent findings on the subject.

2. Nothing will be gained by suppressing and denying the emotions. They should be pulled out of hiding and eyeballed.

3. Do not simply try to drive out bad thoughts. When the unclean spirit was driven out, he later returned to the house and found it empty, swept, and garnished. Such a condition prompted him to take seven other spirits, more wicked than himself, to his original dwelling place. We cannot simply say that we should not be envious, puffed up, rude, selfish, or angry.

4. The bad thoughts that produce negative emotions must be replaced with good thoughts. In Philippians 4:8 we are instructed to think on things that are true, honest, just, pure, lovely, and of good report. Only the proper positive thoughts can drive out and replace the negative thoughts which produce negative emotions.

A WOMAN'S POINT OF VIEW

LOVE ENVIES NOT. If I am perfectly honest, I will have to admit that frequently women are a bit envious of their husbands, especially if they are successful professionals. The husband's career may seem glamorous and fulfilling. Sometimes the wife may feel a tinge of envy when she compares her lot with that of her husband. For some reason her role as a homemaker does not receive the acclaim that it should. If she does have a job outside the home, often it does not have the prestige of her husband's career. If she is perfectly honest, however, she probably would not have his job with all the responsibilities and headaches if it were handed to her on a silver platter.

Sometimes a wife is envious of her husband's hobbies. She very strongly resents the time and the money which he invests. She is not at all interested in possessing his new fishing rod or the gun for herself. If she had them, she would probably not know what to do with either one. But so often she very strongly resents his having them.

I think I can understand the underlying reason for a wife's envy. A husband can devote a great deal of time to his career and be successful in it *if* he makes his wife feel that she is first in his life. He can invest a reasonable amount of time and money in a hobby and not provoke envy *if* his wife is made to feel that she is the queen in his life and more important than anything else he may do.

Sometimes there is envy over the amount of attention which a husband pays to another woman. Sadly, with the current lack of commitment to the marriage vows of fidelity, the envy is often justified. Far too many husbands do show too much attention to other women. They are unfaithful to their vows. On the other hand, some wives are envious of any innocent attention which their husbands pay to other women, whether it be a smile or conversation. In this instance, as in the other, the wife should not feel envious *if* her husband has made her feel that she is first in his life—his true queen who is more important than anyone else.

LOVE VAUNTS NOT ITSELF AND IS NOT PUFFED UP. I have seen both husbands and wives flaunt their abilities or achievements before others at the expense of their mates. If the husband has a good mind and is successful in the use of it, then often the wife tries to make others believe that her mind is sharper. She constantly belittles him. On the other hand, if she is an excellent cook, then he professes to be a gourmet. On and on the story goes as each claims to be better than the other.

Most of the time, bragging or puffing oneself up is indicative of a poor self-esteem. A person who feels secure in the image of himself does not have to resort to bragging or any other inflationary measures to build himself up nor to make him feel more important.

Husbands and wives are their mates' chief cheerleaders. If my husband brags about himself or in any way tries to make himself seem more important than he really is, then perhaps I have not spent enough time trying to reinforce his own self-image. I have more influence on this phase of his personality than any other person on the face of the earth during his adult years. Sometimes he failed to receive this positive reinforcement during his formative childhood years, and he consequently was emotionally and socially handicapped. Although my influence is limited, I can still make a difference by being there to love and support.

LOVE DOES NOT BEHAVE ITSELF UNSEEMLY. Love is not graceless and tactless. We wives do the wrong things many times. We *should* be admonished to do something differently. But please tell us with tact and kindness. Your choice of words and the tone of your voice can either make us feel uplifted and want to try harder or else they can crush us and cause us to feel like a nail driven into a wall until nothing is left. Before you offer constructive criticism, please point out some of our good traits first. We have some.

Please never make me the object of your jokes and ridicule. No person likes to have fun poked at them or have someone make light of deficiencies.

When you become upset, please do not act as a child. Do not fly off in a rage or, on the other hand, seek refuge in protective silence as you pout for days upon end. (I am well aware of the fact that women have become masters in such protective devices.)

Instead of acting out your frustrations by withdrawal or aggression, please sit down with me and tell me how you honestly feel. If vexations are handled properly, they can be resolved and put into the past.

LOVE SEEKS NOT HER OWN. There is no place in marriage for selfishness. There is no way that two selfish individuals can live together in the closeness of the marriage relationship. Neither the husband nor the wife should lose his or her own identity and become a slave to the other.

The fifth chapter of Ephesians reveals the way that God intended for marriage to work. It is to be a sacrificial love with each partner doing everything possible for the betterment of the other, just as Christ loved His bride so much that He gladly gave His life for her. When I sense that my husband loves me to the same degree, it definitely affects my behavior toward him. I cannot do enough to please him.

On the other hand, when husbands and wives approach marriage as a 50-50 contract, the entire atmosphere changes. Whenever I sense that you are demanding your fair share, then the battle line has been drawn. I will do my part and no more.

Quite frankly, I feel that much of the selfishness in today's marriages can be traced to two paychecks in the home. Each has worked hard for the money. The natural instinct is to call it *mine* and *yours* instead of *ours*. "You pay your part of the expenses and I will pay mine. The rest of my check is mine to spend as I please." Selfishness breeds selfishness.

We do not change the way others act by demanding. Instead, we change the manner with which we treat them and they respond in kind. It may be a slow process but the best way to teach unselfishness is to practice it. Eventually it will work. It is far more powerful than ranting or raving over our rights.

LOVE IS NOT EASILY PROVOKED. Anger is undoubtedly the most talked about and also the least understood emotion associated with love and marriage. An improper display of anger probably causes more trouble than any other one factor.

Pick up many women's magazines and they will advise couples to have a good argument to clear the air. Throw things. Shout. Do anything to get the pent-up feelings out of your system.

Once words have been spoken, however, they can never be recalled. Angry words are usually unkind. We can eloquently say we are sorry and try to pull the daggers out, but they leave emotional scars. Once the sense of worth has been attacked, the victim can never again be the same.

Many Christians deplore any display of anger. Instead, we pout. We keep the anger buried so deeply inside that even we are not always aware of its presence. It seems more righteous to say that we have been deeply hurt than to admit anger. Martyrs that we are, we choose to bury the injustice and refrain from even making mention of the incident. We can be so pious.

God was angry—many times. Use your concordance to determine how often He felt this emotion. Christ was angry, too. Claiming that feeling anger is wrong is tantamount to saying that God and Christ sinned. Such is not the case (Hebrews 4:15).

Stated very simply, anger is an irritated emotion. It happens all the time and is just as natural as becoming hungry. Either can become a sin if not handled properly. The secret is found in Ephesians 4:26: "Be ye angry and sin not. Let not the sun go down upon your wrath." Being angry, or having irritated emotions, is only natural. Imbedding those feelings in the subconscious and acting as if they had never existed is wrong. Emotions never die. They smolder in the garbage dump of the mind until they suddenly burst forth in a rage one day, perhaps even years later, when triggered by an insignificant happening. Through inspiration the writer of Ephesians is simply admonishing us to acknowledge the fact that we will become angry, recognize the emotion when we feel it, call it by name, then dissipate the feeling before the day ends. There are a number of ways to lessen the evil effects of anger. Ideally, we have developed communication skills with our mates to the point that we feel free to simply say to one another, "What you said made me feel angry. Let's talk about it." The matter should be settled in a caring, loving way before the day comes to an end. Sometimes it is impossible to do the best. If we cannot talk it over with our mates, we should admit the anger to ourselves. Sometimes we can lessen the effect by writing the grievance on a piece of paper and then burning it. At other times we may vent anger by getting off to ourselves and letting off steam. We most certainly should carry our problem to the throne of God and there admit the anger both to ourselves and to the Father. Then lessen the effects before a night falls upon us. Never allow anger to ferment.

LOVE THINKS NO EVIL. Women have nearly always been prone to delight in collecting trading stamps or in the accumulation of coupons until the time comes for cashing them in.

Just as an accountant enters the figures under the correct column in the ledger, we also feel the prick from some remark or action from our mates and file the hurt in the subconscious part of the mind. Instead of recognizing the emotional hurt and getting rid of it, we collect grievances just as gleefully as a cannibal would save and display a collection of human heads.

For example, our husbands may overlook a birthday or an anniversary. We say nothing but file the offense in our memory banks. Our spouses could make some cutting remark about the way we look. We usually bite our tongues but drop the index card with a full description of our emotional hurts under the proper category in our bad-deed file. One day they may absentmindedly fail to do something they had promised. We lash out with a fury that is completely out of proportion to the offense simply because we have been keeping a record of all past offenses instead of ridding ourselves of the ill feelings as each one arises.

Forgiveness is sweet—both to the one forgiven but most of all to the forgiver. Storing injustices does far more harm to the cup in which they are stored than to the ground on which they may be spilled.

LOVE REJOICES NOT IN INIQUITY. Some people gloat over wrongs. It seems that they would be miserable if they were married to a perfect mate. It wouldn't be fun. There would be nothing over which to argue and complain.

I have done many wrong things. Undoubtedly I will do even more. I realize that I must daily seek forgiveness from God and the one wronged. So many of my mistakes, however, are just that—mistakes in human judgment simply because I am human. Thank you, Don, for being longsuffering and understanding. Thank you for not delighting in the wrongs which I have done and constantly throwing them up in my face, especially in the presence of others. Thank you for your knack of taking one of my bad traits and twisting it into a good one. Only love could make you reach down deeply into my heart and find something good.

A MAN'S POINT OF VIEW

LOVE ENVIES NOT. Because of the vast differences that exist between male and female, the differences in roles, and the added differences in individuals, there could be multitudes of things about which envy could exist. A hard-driving professional man might secretly envy his wife's spare time for clubs, tennis, reading, or other activities to which she has time to devote. A browbeaten salesman might envy his wife's ability to be her own boss. A less-than-successful competitor in the labor market might envy his wife's social success or, if she is also working outside the home, her economic or professional success. He may envy her talent, her personality, or her education. Because competition is a natural quality of life, it is easy for envy to turn to resentment. There may be no desire on his part to exchange places with her, but he resents anything that seems to put him in second place. Genuine love rules out both envy and resentment. According to which type personality a man possesses (A—hard driving and competitive; B—more *laid back*), some men must work harder at conquering these negative emotions than others have to work. His wife can help in large measure by not flaunting her blessings. Her greater earning power or education must be handled very carefully. Her personality must never be used with other men in a way to provoke jealousy from her husband. Like most other things in life, love is a two way street. A husband cannot envy or resent his wife. She may use her gifts wisely, thoughtfully, and lovingly, which in return, will help her husband be genuinely proud of her, thankful for her, and happy to be known as her husband.

LOVE VAUNTS NOT ITSELF AND IS NOT PUFFED UP. It is easy for one to "think himself to be something when he is nothing" (Galatians 6:3). Ego is the center of our being. Like a drowning man grasping at a straw, one will go to almost any length to protect the core of his personality, his sense of self-worth. He will brag about the smallest and most insignificant success or even manufacture such success out of his own imagination. A realization that one is God-made and has great individual worth apart from any accomplishment should be the major factor in conquering these two defects. The Gospel is intended to give one that realization. A loving and supportive wife should be the second most important factor in helping a man overcome these ugly displays. The poor man does not realize what a boor and object of ridicule he is to others when he is trying to make something of accomplishments that are not really there. The real ugliness of the situation is seen in the constant criticism and put down of his wife and his *I-can-top-that* attitude toward anything that would exalt her. Few things hurt a spouse more than these. True love is a servant, not a master. Why must a man criticize his wife's intelligence, cooking, housekeeping, hair, clothes, make-up, or anything else in order to try to exalt himself? He succeeds only in further alienating himself from her and all others before whom he displays such an attitude. Why must he insist he can cook better, dress better, think better, or outperform her in any area? If he can, the proof stands on its own merit without bragging. If he can't, he only makes himself a liar before others. Nothing is gained and everything is lost by such behavior. There is no love where such a disposition exists. It must be conquered. God's grace is available to help win that battle. Husbands, don't let this sin drive away the one who loves you most.

LOVE DOES NOT BEHAVE ITSELF UNSEEMLY. As human beings we are all flawed; there is no one perfect. Spouses usually know the imperfections of each other better than those of anyone. Unseemly behavior is constantly picking at the scabs of these sores. Many of them would heal if only left alone. As we learned earlier, "Love covers a multitude of imperfections both by absorbing and forgiving and by helping shoulder the burden so it will not be so apparent to others." Tell me my faults gently, not with glee. Expose my weakness to me with tears of sympathy, not in the hot words of an argument. If we are not careful, faultfinding can bring a strange sense of satisfaction, and the faultfinder becomes a buzzard whose only desire is to find something rotten. Few men want to go home knowing there is a vulture roosting there. Be a nurse who lovingly binds my wounds and I will love you more deeply for it.

LOVE SEEKS NOT HER OWN. Selfishness and love do not live in the same heart. Sadly, our generation has been bombarded with Satan's lie of *me-ism.* When one's greatest desire is to please and gratify self, everyone else, including God, is relegated to a lower position. The so-called Women's Liberation Movement has called for women to *find fulfillment* in deserting their God-given roles and demanding more authority and power. The materialism of our age has increased the appetite for *things.* The secularization of our society through the philosophy of humanism has greatly affected sexual standards. In too many instances husband and wife remain two instead of becoming the *one flesh* God intended. When a woman resents not only her role as a woman but also her roles of wife and mother because she feels they deprive her of *fulfillment* or the opportunity to do, be, or possess everything she wants, the marriage is on shaky ground. Husbands can help tremendously by recognizing that the wife is both keeper and queen of the home. When subjection is mutual (Ephesians 5:21) and his role is not exercised with a heavy hand; when he puts her wants first in spending money not budgeted to necessities; when he respects her dignity not only as an individual but in the special way a woman possesses dignity; when he realizes that *keep*ing the home does not mean *staying* at home; when he realizes rearing children is also his God-given responsibility; when she sees her subjection to him makes him gentler and sweeter to her—many of the problems of selfishness will be solved.

LOVE IS NOT EASILY PROVOKED. All human beings are subject to provocation to both good and evil. Some, however, are more easily provoked, by nature, than others. Regardless of our temperament we must not allow ourselves to be easily provoked to evil. There are certain words and actions that are the particular weaknesses of our mate. To help our loved one to avoid this sin we should NEVER resort to the use of these. Sometimes as a defense when under criticism, or as a counterattack when we have been wounded, or in a deliberate attempt to strike back for some other reason, we ignite these *flash points*. In such instances we are no more innocent than the one whom we have provoked. Yet, regardless of circumstances, each is responsible for his or her own actions.

The word under consideration here has to do with rage—anger out of control. Anger is not a sin; in fact it is commanded by God (Ephesians 4:26). It may be the catalyst of many good actions. I am as fearful of the spiritual and emotional health of one who denies being angered by anything as I am of the one who seems to be angered by everything. Husbands and wives need to learn the art of communication in order that they may discuss their anger. Prayer is a most successful tool in handling anger. Often anger is merely frustration that can be worked out in some project and completely forgotten.

Rage, however, cannot so easily be dealt with. Work hard at keeping anger from progressing to rage. Rage inflicts deep wounds and leaves ugly scars. Love will do anything possible to avoid rage. The two cannot coexist.

LOVE THINKS NO EVIL. Our imaginations can play terrible tricks on us. With the imperfections we all possess, one can continually dredge mistakes from the life of the other until he can imagine that nothing but evil is there. From real mistakes we can take flights of fantasy with the imagination to any destination we desire. An imagination can become as real to us as an actual occurrence. When I allow myself the liberty of letting my imagination run wild, I am asking for trouble and heartache. I have *no right* to suppose or accuse my wife of *anything* for which I do not have proof. Our relationship is to be of such nature that I trust her implicitly and completely. Without such faith our marriage cannot endure. Today's mobile society and work patterns mean that husbands and wives are separated daily for long hours and in many instances for days or weeks at a time. It must never enter my mind to question my wife's fidelity.

I cannot think evil is the motive that prompts any of her actions. To question her motives for anything she does for me, our children, our friends, or anyone else is simply unchristian conduct on my part. I must attribute to every action only the highest and noblest of intentions unless I know them to be otherwise. That's what love is.

LOVE REJOICES NOT IN INIQUITY. Of all the possible ways to deal with the mistakes of another's life, taking delight in them is the worst. Truly, sin must be dealt with and God prescribes the means and the manner. Iniquity separates us from God (Isaiah 59:1,2); it also separates us from one another. How should husbands and wives deal with the matter of sin in their spouse's life? As Christians we must lovingly communicate about the matter. Whether I am wrong or have been wronged, it is the duty of love to make the first move toward forgiveness and reconciliation (Matthew 5:38-40; 18:15-18). These verses make it clear that neither party has the right to expect the other to take the initiative. Rather than the approach of who is right and who is wrong, love says, "I want to be the first to make up." God set the example for us by taking the first step toward reconciliation even though we were the offending party.

While it is true that actions are committed by people and thus wrong actions mean people are wrong, love desires to deal with the wrongness of the action. Correct that and the person is no longer wrong. It is much easier and more objective to deal directly with actions than with people. Love demands that I help bear the burden of sin (Galatians 6:1,2). When love is absent and there is rejoicing in iniquity, sin is made bare and laid naked to be made a spectacle.

Many things which husbands and wives treat as if they were iniquities are simply the mistakes of judgment and shortcomings of daily living that characterize us all. In fact, many a spouse is more upset over these than over actual sin. Love does not rejoice in or gloat over the imperfections of a mate. Instead, it takes into account that we are all human and makes special allowances for the partner's *bad days*. Occasionally, everyone *gets up on the wrong side of the bed*. We should not even count those days.

My wife lives with a sinful man. She knows it, I know it, and God knows it (Romans 3:23). I do not want her to overlook my sin. I want her to be sensitive, caring, and loving as she helps me make wrongs right. In the short run she will thereby help make me a better husband and in the long run save my soul (James 5:19-20). My wife also lives with a very imperfect man. Without wounding my pride or destroying my ego, I want her to help me improve both as an accountable being in society and as her husband. When she does that, she is the winner in so many ways. It is part of our basic makeup to love those who help us feel better about ourselves. That is both the power and reward of love. It is self-perpetuating because each always produces the other. Those who rejoice in the failures of their mates kill the goose that lays the golden egg. They kill in their marriage the very thing that produces what they sought from the marriage to begin with.

IN CONCLUSION

1. Emotions often result from perceptions rather than facts.

2. Harboring negative emotions is dangerous to spiritual, emotional, and physical health.

3. We can rid ourselves of negative emotions by learning to deal with them properly.

4. True love is the formula for dealing properly with our emotions.

5. The real glue of every happy and successful marriage is the true love that is described in 1 Corinthians 13.

SUGGESTIONS FOR CLASS DISCUSSION

1. Do you agree or disagree with the statement that the underlying cause for the breakup of most marriages can be traced to negative emotions? What are some manifestations?

2. Emotions are a person's feelings based upon his perception of an event or circumstances instead of the facts. Give concrete examples.

3. If emotions are produced by thoughts, what is the answer to controlling emotions? (Note Galatians 6:7; Proverbs 23:7; 25:28.)

4. Cite examples of the influence of emotions on physical health.

5. Discuss the five suggestions given for dealing with negative emotions. Add to this list.

6. Compare viewpoints of both a man and a woman on these characteristics of love:
   a. Love envies not.
   b. Love vaunts not itself and is not puffed up.
   c. Love does not behave itself unseemly.
   d. Love seeks not her own.
   e. Love is not easily provoked.
   f. Love rejoices not in iniquity.